A Classical Guide to Narration

A Classical Guide to Narration

by Jason Barney

....

CiRCE
Concord, NC

Published in the USA
by the CiRCE Institute
@2020 Jason Barney
ISBN: 978-1-7347853-2-6

For information:
CiRCE Institute
81 McCachern Blvd.
Concord, NC 28025
www.circeinstitute.org

Cover design by Graeme Pitman
Layout by Courtney Sanford

Printed in the United States of America.

TABLE OF CONTENTS

....

FOREWORD
by Kevin Clark

If this book's only achievement is to introduce the practice of narration as a concrete and practical way forward in the search for a distinctly classical pedagogy, it will be a gift to classical educators across the renewal. But it accomplishes so much more. It holds Charlotte Mason's educational philosophy, the classical model, and even contemporary research into the science of learning within a single vision. In order to grasp the significance of this achievement, it is necessary briefly to view the principles inspiring the renewal of classical education in light of contemporary developments.

The classical model of education flows from key insights about the proper order of learning: The path to wisdom begins in wonder, growth in virtue starts with good habits, and liberal arts learning proceeds from imitation. The renewal of classical education in our own day began by restoring wisdom and virtue to their proper place as the twofold goal of education and by recovering the liberal arts—especially the language arts of the trivium—as the curriculum best suited to that end. In recent years, classical educators have become increasingly interested in reflecting on the day-to-day practice of teaching and learning.

Thus pedagogy has taken its place alongside curriculum and vision as key elements in a robust classical model of education.

This renewed interest in pedagogy reflects a larger cultural trend in education. From so-called twenty-first-century education initiatives to the application of cognitive science to the study of how people learn, we are in the midst of an instructional revolution. It is too early to predict how things will turn out, but the emergent model is student-centered and employs adaptive technology to individualize instruction. Setting criticism aside, it is important to note the principles driving this development, namely, that instruction must address the capacities and learning needs of students, that students themselves must do the work of learning if learning is to stick, and that the content of learning must be interesting. While some classical educators have responded to this emergent model by asserting a teacher-centered, direct-instruction approach, others have turned to the great tradition of liberal arts education and are discovering surprising resonances within these contemporary trends.

Like the emergent contemporary model, the classical model also proceeds from an understanding of the student, the curriculum, and the practice of learning. While it affirms the insights discovered by contemporary research and reflection, however, it offers a more robust vision. First, classical learning takes a child's nature as the starting point for instruction. The liberal arts of language and mathematics are designed to cultivate a child's innate capacity for communicating, reasoning, and learning. Second, the classical curriculum appeals to a child's sense of wonder by directing their attention to the inexhaustible sources of wonder themselves—the creation, the story of human history, the great literary tradition, and the Word of God. Finally, classical instruction engages students in the work of learning, starting with what a child delights in—imitative practice—and culminating in the free and productive use of knowledge and skill.

The book you hold now shows how adopting narration brings

all of these strands together. With respect to the classical model's insights about the order of learning, it shows how the practice of narration evokes wonder; cultivates virtuous habits like attention, respect, and perfect execution; and engages students in the imitative practices of the liberal arts. Because children naturally love to tell back what they have heard, narration also addresses the pedagogical insights recently discovered by educational research and more deeply expressed in the tradition. Along the way, this book also shows how Charlotte Mason's insights draw from and fit within, the same great liberal arts tradition as the classical model of education itself. This common heritage provides a way forward for classical and Charlotte Mason educators alike to work together and to learn from each other. My hope is that by providing a classical guide to the basic practice of narration, this book will not simply create a breakthrough for classical education; it may well spark an educational renaissance.

INTRODUCTION

To many of my readers, the practice of narration needs no introduction. Others, however, will be hearing of the practice for the first time. In either case, the best introduction may be a careful description of the practice itself as presented in Chapter One alongside a consideration of its benefits from the perspective of a Christian worldview, the classical tradition, and modern learning science (Chapter Two).

Nevertheless, readers of either type may be interested by persons as well as things. And so, my own story of encountering the practice of narration, followed by the more important story of Charlotte Mason, the discoverer of narration in its full power as a tool of learning, may also be fitting introductions to this powerful teaching practice. This is not to mention the fact that telling a couple of stories—one more recent providing the inciting force behind the author's choice of topic, and the second a short biography, all too rarely told, of an increasingly popular modern educational philosopher—seems like the perfect introduction to a guidebook on narration.

My Story of Practicing Narration

My path to classical education coincided with my introduction to the practice of narration. While looking for a job my senior year at Wheaton College, I happened upon a young classical school nearby that was one of a handful of schools across the nation blending the classical tradition with the philosophy and practices of Charlotte Mason.

When I arrived for a visit, I was ushered in to observe a Bible class of fourth and fifth graders who were reading the book of Jeremiah. After the teacher read aloud a chapter of an intense prophetic oracle, she asked the students to close their Bibles and then called on a student to narrate. I was astonished at the fluency with which a young boy told back much of the obscure poetic language of the passage. I vividly remember thinking to myself, "I'm a fairly bright college student with a double major in English and Ancient Languages and a minor in Bible, and I don't think I could have told back from Jeremiah nearly as well as this boy did."

Looking back, I'm fairly certain that the power of narration as a teaching tool, as well as the quality of discussion and overall learning that result from it, were major factors in my own journey into classical education. I had no idea that young children could engage with ideas at this level. I had previously planned on going into pastoral ministry, so finding classical education led to a major change in my personal career trajectory.

I interned for the rest of that year with the fifth grade class and began teaching Latin and logic. The year after graduation, I split the homeroom sixth grade teaching responsibilities with another teacher and received training in implementing Charlotte Mason's teaching philosophy from Bill and Maryellen St. Cyr, the founders and leaders of Ambleside Schools International, a coalition of schools devoted to applying Charlotte Mason's philosophy today. In addition to my own research into Charlotte

Mason and the classical tradition, Bill and Maryellen deserve credit for many of the practical suggestions I will encourage in this book.[1]

How do I know that narration is effective for long term learning? A notable memory from a couple of years into my teaching practice clinched it for me. One of the literature books in our eighth grade curriculum was C. S. Lewis' classic *The Great Divorce*, a dense and difficult (but gripping!) dream-like tale of an encounter with the realities of heaven and hell.

I had six students in my class, and I remember that one of the first assignments we did was a written narration. After setting up the text, I read aloud the first two chapters of the book. Then I asked them to write a narration of the beginning of *The Great Divorce*. After a couple of groans, they immediately began writing on loose-leaf paper. As the period came to a close, I assigned the task of finishing their narration for homework that night without consulting their book. Each of them came back the next day with 3–4 sides of writing as a testament to their vivid memory of the storyline, including many of the exact details.

The school year proceeded as normal until exams came along. Because of our practice of narration, the school did not encourage students to study for exams; the fact that they attended well to lessons and narrated regularly should have ensured that they knew and remembered in a way that reflected their work throughout the semester. Exams, the school believed, were simply an opportunity to show what the students knew. Well, for that particular literature exam, which happened to occur exactly three months from the first day of school when I had assigned that first written narration, the prompt was to tell back the first two chapters of *The Great Divorce*. Now you should know that none of them had reread or studied it at all since that initial read.

---

1. Maryellen is a contributor to *When Children Love to Learn: A Practical Application of Charlotte Mason's Philosophy for Today*, ed. Elaine Cooper (Wheaton: Crossway, 2004), a valuable resource for those looking for a more general overview of how to apply Charlotte Mason's philosophy in a classroom setting.

In grading those exams, I went back to compare them with the students' first written narration from three months before, and without exception, every one of those students had been able to tell back as thoroughly, if not more thoroughly, than their first written narration. So powerful is the practice of narration for locking content in long-term memory!

So you can see that my experience of classical education was closely connected with the practice of narration from the very start. And more than ten years of implementing it and seeing it faithfully practiced has convinced me of its effectiveness, as well as the fact that, as a teaching practice, it is a central mode of the classical liberal arts tradition and therefore worthy of being implemented in classical schools across the country. That's why I have written this book: to help other classical educators rediscover it and implement it in their own classrooms.

Charlotte Mason

Charlotte Mason was a late nineteenth, early twentieth wcentury British educator, who first adopted narration as a central teaching practice and articulated a philosophy of learning that accounted for its value. She was born in Bangor in 1842, the only child of a Liverpool merchant.[2] Her family was not rich, and the American Civil War put serious financial strain on the Liverpool cotton trade.[3] Added to this was the tragedy of her mother's death in 1858, followed shortly thereafter by her father's. Left alone in the world at the age of sixteen with nothing but a notion "that teaching was the thing to do, and above all the teaching of poor children," she joined the Home and Colonial Society for the training of early childhood teachers, the first and only college like it in England at the time.[4]

---

2. Essex Cholmondeley, *The Story of Charlotte Mason (1842-1923)*, 2nd ed. (Cambridge: Child Light, 2000), vi, 1–2.
3. Ibid., 5.
4. Ibid., 4–5.

Here she met Mr. Dunning, a lecturer in education at the college, from whom she first learned of the history of education and with whom she kept up a correspondence after she took a post at the Davison School in 1861.[5] Perhaps it was from him that she first encountered the ideas of the classical liberal arts tradition in readings from Plato, Quintilian, and John Locke. In fact, in a letter to a college friend during her first year of teaching she wrote:

> It is extremely interesting to have the different stages of educational progress in the old books and old apparatus ... All that Mr Dunning has ever told us about the history of education is exemplified here. I am happy in my work, I have such interesting children.[6]

Mason's deep appreciation and reverence for young children began early, as did her conviction that *all* children could *and should* share in the riches of a liberal arts education. But she also grew up in a time when movements to advance education for the poor had already been gaining steam. The British and Foreign School Society had been founded by Joseph Lancaster in 1810 followed shortly thereafter by Andrew Bell's National School Society in 1811; then came the London Infant School Society in 1824, founded by Robert Owen.[7]

In 1863, Charlotte Mason was awarded a First Class certificate from the Home and Colonial Training College for her studies in the theory and practice of education.[8] After over ten years of teaching at the Davison School and a sabbatical of sorts in Europe for her ill health, she took a position at the Bishop Otter College as a lecturer in education, hygiene and physiology as

---

5. Ibid., 6–7.
6. As quoted in Cholmondeley, *The Story of Charlotte Mason*, 7.
7 Ibid., vii. Charlotte Mason's own college was founded in 1836 to address the ne.ed for trained teachers and governesses for the middle class along with the Governesses' Benevolent Institution in 1848.
8. Ibid., 7–8.

well as the role of Mistress of Method at the college's practicing school.[9] This appointment may have come about because of three long letters she wrote proposing "a state scheme of education" guided by the principle "a liberal education for all."[10]

During her years of teaching, Mason had been, in her own words, "reading a good deal of philosophy and *education* at the time, for [she] thought with the enthusiasm of a young teacher that *education* should regenerate the world."[11] From her practice as a teacher and her reading in the philosophy of education, both ancient and modern thinkers (as can be seen from the quotations in her books), she had come to a few convictions that would be foundational for the practice of narration. First, she came to believe that "the mind of a child takes or rejects according to its needs" and that:

> In taking or rejecting, the mind was functioning for its own nourishment; that the mind, in fact, requires sustenance as does the body, in order that it increase and be strong; but because the mind is not to be measured or weighed but is spiritual, so its sustenance must be spiritual too, must, in fact, be ideas (in the Platonic sense of images) ....[12]

It was here too that she came to her view of knowledge as what a person "assimilated, [that] which his mind has acted upon." This view of the mind as a spiritual organism that must be fed on appropriate sources, like "living books" and the beauty of the world around it, prepared the way for narration as the method of ensuring a steady mental diet.

Second, though, was her recognition of the laws or principles governing a child's attention. Her description of

---

9. Ibid., 9, 12.
10. Ibid.
11. As quoted in Cholmondeley, *The Story of Charlotte Mason*, 10. This wry comment on her own youthful enthusiasm comes from her sixth and final volume *An Essay Toward a Philosophy of Education* (published in 1922), "essay" meaning in the old sense, "a trial, or attempt." Mason participated in the optimism of the modern era, and, it would seem, in the chastening or humbling afforded by the First World War.
12. Ibid., 10.

how she came upon these ideas that would lead her more immediately to the practice of narration is suggestive and enlightening, if not as detailed as we might wish:

> It is difficult to explain how I came to a solution of a puzzling problem—how to secure attention. Much observation of children, various incidents from one's general reading, the recollection of my own child-hood and the consideration of my present habits of mind brought me to the recognition of certain laws of mind, by working in accordance with which the steady attention of children of any age and any class in society is insured, week in, week out—attention, not affected by distracting circumstances ....[13]

The details of the practice of narration are the solution she was referring to here, and it can be clearly seen that she does not cite the classical tradition directly or current educational practices as the source of her solution to the problem of attention. Charlotte Mason felt that she had hit upon something new with the practice of narration.

However, clear connections to earlier authors, like John Locke and Quintilian, in her discussions of narration seem to indicate that she was drawing from traditional practices of the grammatical and rhetorical tradition.[14] Her chief innovation was globalizing these exercises into a meta-practice for learning content in any subject and combining it with a primarily book-based method.[15]

The rest of Charlotte Mason's history is more well known because it is more public. After retiring from her work at Bishop

13. As quoted in Cholmondeley, *The Story of Charlotte Mason*, 11.

14. Narrating stories from a text was an early staple of the *progymnasmata* or preparatory exercises of the rhetorical tradition. See Chapter One's section on "Narration as a Traditional Teaching Practice" and Chapter Six, "Narration in the Liberal Arts Tradition," for further discussion of the practice's relationship to the classical tradition.

15. Erasmus and Comenius had arguably already recommended the retelling of the teacher's explanation or lecture as a global teaching practice, on which see the quotations with references in Karen Glass' *Know and Tell: The Art of Narration* (Scotts Valley: Karen Glass, 2018), 16.

Otter College and traveling for a couple years, she moved to Bradford in north England to work at the middle school there and have more free time to write.[16] Aside from publishing five volumes of geography readers, she gave a series of lectures to raise money for a church building project in 1885. The response was so great that she published them as *Home Education,* and by 1887, the Parents' National Educational Union was started.[17] To further the work of the union, a periodical called the *Parents' Review* was begun in 1891 followed by a House of Education at Charlotte Mason's new home in Ambleside. This became the training ground for governesses and teachers in her methods, and a practicing school called the Parents' Review School was started immediately to provide teachers with practical experience.[18]

The rest—as they say—is history. Five volumes later and a few decades of leading a growing organization with an international following left a legacy of educational thought that has been stirring revival movements ever since. Among the many Charlotte Mason revivals worthy of mention is Susan Schaeffer Macaulay's Child-Light and her stirring appeal in *For the Children's Sake: Foundations of Education for Home and School.*[19] But perhaps the key distinctive practice of Charlotte Mason's educational movement was narration.[20] While other practices may come to mind more readily for some Charlotte Mason enthusiasts—say nature study, habit training, or "living books,"—the core practice at the heart of her prescribed method, the one with the most far-reaching application, is narration.

But why a guidebook on narration when Charlotte Mason's

---

16. Cholmondeley, *The Story of Charlotte Mason*, 14.

17. Ibid., 16. It first started as a series of local branches of Parents' Educational Unions in various cities like Bradford, London (3 by 1891), Cheltenham, etc., before being renamed in 1892 (see 30, 41).

18. Ibid., 42–3. It was later renamed the Parents' Union school.

19. Published by Crossway (Wheaton, 1984).

20. Compare Maryellen's comment in *When Children Love to Learn*, 128: "Narration is considered the sum total of Charlotte Mason's philosophy and practice of education. She had discovered narration as the foundation stone of learning."

works are readily accessible?[21] A few answers might be given. First, while Mason mentions narration often, her comments are sporadic and not easily pinned down in terms of application to a modern school setting. Second, since narration is so counter-intuitive in the modern era, a guide to its implementation serves the purpose of helping other schools avoid pitfalls along the path. Schools are conservative creatures and will be reticent to adopt a new teaching method without a carefully plotted course of action for successful implementation. Third, and lastly, many classical educators may be less likely to wade into Charlotte Mason's Victorian prose to hunt out old practices without a modern guide pointing the way. And after all, narration is a story worth retelling.

---

21. This question is compounded by the presence of Karen Glass' helpful and inspiring book, *Know and Tell: The Art of Narration*, published just a couple of years ago. Hers is an invaluable resource for using narration, especially for home educators. As a practitioner at a classical school, I have written this guide to function as a companion piece focused on application in a school setting.

Chapter One
....

WHAT IS NARRATION?

Narration is a teaching practice in which students are asked to communicate back the substance of content they have learned. It has two core components: 1) the exposure of the student to content, and 2) the student's narration of that content.

In this way, narration has an elegant simplicity to it, as well as a ready adaptability. In a classical classroom, this will most often come in the reading of a passage of a classic text followed by a student's spoken or written narration. But it could also begin with the presentation of a beautiful painting, a skillful lecture or explanation, or the demonstration of some train of reasoning on a whiteboard as in a geometric proof. The student's narration could then come through an artistic imitation of his own, the solution of a similar mathematical problem, or the write-up of a science lab report after its completion.[22] Narration is adaptable to the nature of the content and the various means of communication.

At the same time, with all this variability, there is the essential

---

22. Karen Glass recommends illustration and dramatic narrations, citing the PNEU schools, in *Know and Tell*, 46-50. The math and science examples here illustrate how the essence of narration can be employed in diverse subjects and advanced material. See further the discussion of the quadrivium in Chapter Six.

simplicity of the two components: exposure and imitation of content. Some might even say that narration mirrors the core of the teaching act itself.[23] The teacher has in her possession specific content that she wishes to teach. She exposes the student to that content, then he responds by communicating his understanding of that content back to the teacher.

Narration as Assimilation and Assessment

Through the student's communication of the content, at least two things are happening. First, the student is himself assimilating the content. By being forced to articulate his understanding of what he perceived, he has to think through the content in a way that solidifies his own grasp of it. The new knowledge crystalizes in his memory.

Charlotte Mason used the term "assimilation" frequently in her works to describe what occurs in the mind during narration. She connected assimilation to the image of how the body consumes food and derives energy from it through the digestion process. This organic growth and sustenance of the body was, she thought, the proper metaphor for the mind's feeding on knowledge. As she expresses in the synopsis of her philosophy of education, published in her final volume *Towards a Philosophy of Education*:

> We hold that the child's mind is no mere sac to hold ideas; but is rather if the figure may be allowed, a spiritual organism, with an appetite for all knowledge.

---

23. This account of the act of teaching is comparable to John Milton Gregory's definition of teaching as "the systematic inculcation of knowledge" vis-à-vis training as "the systematic development and cultivation of the powers of mind and body" (*The Seven Laws of Teaching*, Moscow, ID: Canon Press, 2017, reprint from 1st edition, 1886; p. 10). Later on he describes teaching more basically as "the communication of knowledge": "It is the painting in another's mind the mental picture in one's own—the shaping of a pupil's thought and understanding to the comprehension of some truth which the teacher knows and wishes to communicate."

> This is its proper diet, with which it is prepared to
> deal; and which it can digest and assimilate as the
> body does foodstuffs.[24]

The metaphor of assimilation thus encourages us to think of the mind as living and organic, equipped with its own natural processes for sustaining and developing its own life. Narration is like sitting down to a meal during which one imbibes knowledge and ideas. Without such a process of mental digestion, content is not stored in long-term memory.

As we'll see, both ancient wisdom and modern research have confirmed this function of narration. When a person does the active work of retrieving content from their memory by communicating it, their memories are strengthened and forgetting is, to a large extent, prevented. In a way, we could say that the act of narration is learning itself since it is the act that produces a lasting record in the brain. Knowledge forgotten is not knowledge at all. As Charlotte Mason says, "Whatever a child or grown-up person can tell, that we may be sure he knows, and what he cannot tell, he does not know."[25]

In a similar vein, she calls narration the "act of knowing," going on to comment:

> We are all aware, alas, what a monstrous quantity
> of printed matter has gone into the dustbin of our
> memories, because we have failed to perform that
> quite natural and spontaneous "act of knowing," as
> easy to a child as breathing and, if we would believe
> it, comparatively easy to ourselves.[26]

Narration enables that act of the mind by which knowledge is assimilated rather than discarded into the "dustbin" of forgotten content.

---

24. Charlotte Mason, *Towards a Philosophy of Education* (Radford, VA: Wilder, 2008), 10.
25. Ibid., 133.
26. Ibid., 80.

The second thing that is occurring in narration is that the student's communication of the content, in whatever form that takes, provides the teacher with data about the nature of the student's understanding. Narration is therefore an assessment—an opportunity for the teacher to assess a student's learning. The quality of the narration reveals how a student has assimilated or interpreted the content.

Because of this, it has all the possibilities of an assessment for informing a teacher's interventions to promote further learning. For instance, after a narration, a teacher could correct a student's telling at a key point, clarify something the child didn't understand, or ask questions to bring out a deeper understanding of the content. Modern education has called this a formative assessment because it is intended to form or shape the ongoing process of learning, not simply to judge a student's accomplishment for the purpose of an abstract symbol system like a grade.[27]

Judging is the primary purpose of a summative assessment, which certainly has its place, at least for as long as it will be desirable in our society to differentiate degrees of successful learning or levels of accomplishment in students. Yet in a way, even in this case, at the end of a term or year of school, the grade is also intended to form or inform the student's learning process going forward. Do they need to work harder or study more effectively? Should they take this course or that course next? What fields should they go into?

Narration is both the assimilation of content and its assessment, whether initial or final. But it is perhaps important to differentiate narration from other forms of assimilation or assessment because the way we have been talking about it has up to this point been so general as to make narration sound like a

27. For example, Glenn Whitman and Ian Kelleher in *Neuroteach: Brain Science and the Future of Education* describe the term "formative" as indicating that these assessments "help form memory, rather than judge it" (Lanham, MD: Rowman and Littlefield, 2016), 85. They further note: "Research suggests that frequent testing aids memory consolidation and recall, but these should be formative assessments, either for no grade, a low grade or graded on effort. ... The other benefit of formative assessment is the feedback it gives the teacher about how both the class and individual students are doing so that they can alter their teaching or pacing accordingly" (85).

teaching practice that all teachers are doing all the time anyway. This is emphatically not the case.

Distinguishing Narration from Other Teaching Practices

In tests and exams students are often asked to recount something of the content they have been previously exposed to, but they are often asked to do so in formats that are markedly different from the nature of the content when they were first exposed to it. For instance, the coherent historical account of a time period that students read in their textbook is broken up into a series of unrelated multiple choice or true-false questions from various subsections. While such a test does require a student to recount facts or inferences from the content, it has reshaped and dissected that content into a series of unrelated propositions.

Narration, on the other hand, involves communicating content as a connected storyline or train of thought—something that hangs together and in which one point flows naturally into another. This is the natural way that the mind absorbs new content, as one thing leading to another. But some forms of testing or questioning break up the content into discrete bits and ask questions concerning disconnected facts. The aim in this sort of practice is still to judge a student's understanding of the content and inform the continuing learning process. However, this is not narration because it does not allow for the student's recitation of the content in full.

> Advanced narration techniques may involve students narrating only part of what they were exposed to, but they are still asked to tell that part fully. So by "in full" we do not mean that narration must always be comprehensive of all the content to which they were exposed but that what they do tell is continuous and full, rather than piecemeal.

Discrete questioning, as in a multiple-choice exam or a teacher's rapid-fire comprehension questions, is analytical rather than synthetic.[28] It breaks apart the content into facts rather than putting it together into a story.[29] This is why the word "narration" is used, which comes from the Latin word for story telling (*narrāre*).

The other key difference is the amount of time between a student's narration and her initial exposure to the content she is narrating back. Narration as a teaching practice should be required immediately after exposure to the content, or in students who are well-versed in the practice, at least the next day. Of course, one confusing factor is that future "narrations" of some or all of the same content might follow this initial one, both by way of in-class review and in a later test or exam. But the first narration after initial exposure is essential for securing the benefits we will discuss later, especially that of "arresting forgetting."

The practice of narration is therefore quite different from the old standard model of unit planning: ongoing exposure to content with very little student interaction followed by studying or cramming, and a final test. Cram, test, forget.

Instead, narration involves the immediate assimilation of

---

28. I owe this language to Karen Glass, *Know and Tell*, 22-25. She expresses well the value of this aspect of narration:

> Contemporary educational practices, which often require students to produce bits of specific information, are frequently fragmented in nature. Isolated pieces of information are required as answers to questions. However, truly great and innovative thinking must include the ability to synthesize knowledge. This has been recognized by scholars and thinkers for centuries. Synthetic thinking, at its foundation, is the development of a personal relationship with the material being learned, so that the pupil achieves a level of familiarity with it that allows at least the potential for connecting what she is learning to things she has learned before or might learn in the future (24).

29. In his book *Something They Will Not Forget: A Handbook for Classical Teachers* (Concord, NC: CiRCE, 2018) Joshua Gibbs criticizes the modern focus on testing the memorization of "objective" facts as opposed to subjective responses like essays. The claims articulated here cut across this important problem since narration embraces facts and data within the context of a broader story but without focusing on them piecemeal. In this solution, narration bridges the gap from knowledge of objective facts to the flowering of subjective responses that constitutes true wisdom.

content and assessment of student learning. Students are required to recreate the content in their minds as a continuous story right from the get-go.

Narration as a Traditional Teaching Practice

It might be fairly said that narration, in its many forms, has been a mainstay of traditional education. Before the modern era students were regularly asked to tell or write in detail the content that they had heard or read. Narration provided the simple and natural accountability for students' absorption of content.

Up through the nineteenth century in America or Britain, for instance, students might be expected to recite or report on the previous day's lesson or the reading they had done at home. Paper was not cheap, and students telling what they knew (and leaving out what they didn't know) was the easiest and most efficient way to hold students accountable for learning and to gather data about where to proceed next.

An example of this can be found in Fred Scott and Joseph Denney's *Elementary English Composition*, published in 1900, which refers to something very much like what Charlotte Mason calls "narration"under the name of "recitation":

> We are often asked in recitation to tell about a certain subject, without the help of direct questions. Then, unless we can recall definite things about the subject and the order in which things come, we are likely to be confused. In order to make a good recitation in history, for example, we must notice, as we study the lesson the first time, what the topics are and what things are said under each topic. Then when we are called to recite we shall be able to remember better

the definite statements about each topic, and not mix these statements up.[30]

This advice for students, with practice exercises listed following, illustrates the use of "recitation" in classrooms in America prior to this time. In fact, it existed as a standard school exercise for grammar and rhetoric teachers in the classical era, and, in entirely oral form, back into pre-literate traditional societies.[31]

For instance, Quintilian, the first-century Roman rhetoric teacher, who wrote the most extensive work on education we have from the ancient world, recommends it for the early training of an orator:

> Let boys learn, then, to relate orally the fables of Aesop, which follow next after the nurse's stories, in plain language, not rising at all above mediocrity, and afterwards to express the same simplicity in writing. Let them learn, too, to take to pieces the verses of the poets and then to express them in different words, and afterwards

---

30. Fred Scott and Joseph Denney, *Elementary English Composition* (Boston and Chicago: Allyn and Bacon, 1900), 22. The authors Scott and Denney, professors of Rhetoric at the University of Michigan and Ohio State University respectively, can be assumed to have a fair sense of the teaching practices in secondary schools current at the time. They go on to discuss the "oral abstract" in which a pupil is asked to read up "outside of class a magazine article, or a chapter of a book, which treats fully some point that the text-book barely mentions, and to be ready to state orally at a later recitation the ideas which he has gained from the reading" (27).

In the same way, they discuss an "oral reproduction": "Sometimes the reading assigned to us is so important or interesting that we are expected to reproduce in our own words every one of the principal ideas in it" (28–29). Again, this illustrates the presence of narration as a mainstay in traditional education, even if it was not being applied systematically as a core pedagogical method in the way that Charlotte Mason did.

31. The only way to perpetuate a story or wisdom tradition in a pre-literate culture would have been to tell it to others and have it retold by the learner. This process with successive tellings, retellings, and corrections would have necessarily constituted the main element in education in oral cultures. See, for instance, Walter Ong's *Orality and Literacy: The Technologizing of the Word* (London and New York: Methuen, 1982).

to represent them, somewhat boldly, in a paraphrase, in which it is allowable to abbreviate or
embellish certain parts, provided that the sense
of the poet be preserved. He who shall successfully perform this exercise, which is difficult even
for accomplished professors, will be able to learn
anything.[32]

The grammarian, or teacher of reading, writing, and the
interpretation of authors, was the one who was supposed
to apply this pre-exercise or *progymnasmata*. Notice how
Quintilian already had a sense that the ability to learn itself is
tied up with this teaching practice. But such exercises had been
established even before Quintilian. As George A. Kennedy, one
of the leading experts on the history of rhetoric, puts it:

The earliest surviving treatment of progymnasmata is the work of Aelius Theon, a teacher in
Alexandria in the middle of the first century after
Christ. In Theon's method of teaching a passage
was read aloud and students were first required
to listen and try to write it out from memory;
after gaining skill in doing this they were given a
short passage and asked to paraphrase it and to
develop and amplify it, or seek to refute it.[33]

It's worth noting that the main goals in such exercises are
primarily fluency in speech or writing and the imitation of
the style of a notable author.[34] Before Charlotte Mason's time,
Renaissance and early modern educators like Erasmus and
Comenius had already shifted the purpose to the acquisition

---

32. Quintilian, *Institutes of Oratory* 1.9.2–3, trans. John Selby Watson, ed. Curtis
Dozier and Lee Honeycutt (Creative Commons, 2015), 49–50.
33. George A. Kennedy, *Classical Rhetoric and its Christian and Secular Tradition from Ancient to Modern Times*, 2nd ed., revised and enlarged (University of
North Carolina, 1999), 26–27.
34. On the importance of imitation or *mimesis*, see ibid., 133.

of knowledge, and she likely followed their move.[35]

Why Was Narration Abandoned?

We could surmise a few reasons for why the educational establishment abandoned narration as a teaching practice. Perhaps, as class sizes grew to accommodate more and more students because of the crowding of cities after the Industrial Revolution, it was felt that a long recital by a student was inefficient and time consuming. Since this could not be done for each student, and one student's narration could not adequately stand for the progress of the whole class, other more "effective" grading methods were devised. This had the unfortunate effect of crowding out the regular student interaction with the content that had been standard up to that point (at least in good classrooms).

At the same time, it could be that the new ideas of the Enlightenment era may also have inspired a focus upon discrete facts and the analytical intellect to the detriment of the synthetic and more holistic storytelling of narration. Likewise, we can understand how the impulse to standardize and quantify, coming into its own in the modern era, could have had the effect of crowding out of consideration practices like narration that refuse easy systematization. For this very reason, narration is arguably more human and embodied than other discrete or analytical teaching practices.

---

35. Erasmus had said that "the master must not omit to set as an exercise the reproduction of what he has given to the class. It involves time and trouble to the teacher, I know well, but it is essential. A literal reproduction of the matter taught is, of course, not required—but the substance of it presented in the pupil's own way" (as quoted in Glass, *Know and Tell*, 16). Notice the focus on the "substance" of "the matter taught" rather than style or skill.

Likewise, Comenius recommended that "every pupil should acquire the habit of acting as a teacher. This will happen if, after the teacher has fully demonstrated and expounded something, the pupil himself is immediately required to give a satisfactory demonstration and exposition of the same thing in the same manner" (ibid.).

NOTA BENE These comments are necessarily general and speculative, since there are no major studies of the use and disuse of narration in education, especially in the way we have defined it. However, as a default mode, in the classical tradition, teachers often expected students to tell what they knew in a long-form connected format, whereas today in general, teachers are wary of this and are more comfortable questioning about discrete facts, either aloud or in a multiple-choice format.

I would add that I am certainly not claiming that traditional education regularly implemented narration according to all the detailed specifics that we will recommend here. My recommendations represent a refinement of the practice of narration based on Charlotte Mason's development of the tradition and the findings of modern research. The how and when of narration matter for optimizing student learning, in all the practical specifics of what the teacher says, does, and expects.

The fact that traditional educators often used narration does not mean that they necessarily used the practice well. So, I should not be heard as making a blanket statement in praise of traditional educators and to the detriment of modern educators.

CHAPTER TWO

WHY PRACTICE NARRATION?

I have already spoken of narration's simplicity and adaptability as well as its traditional use and abandonment in the modern era, but for some educators, these may be strokes against it rather than in its favor. Modern educators may still feel that narration is too time-consuming, that it reflects an antiquated focus on book learning, or that it does not involve the class as actively in the learning process as multi-sensory, tech-savvy PowerPoint lectures with periodic buzzer quizzes built in.

So why should we practice narration? Of course, classical educators will be intrigued by the claim that narration was the traditional default mode of education. If convinced, the very fact that it is old may be enough for them. Tried and true and therefore worth trying again! And all the more so since it is strikingly different from the standard *modus operandi* in modern education.

My main contention for the practice of narration is that it is a natural educational tool—in the sense that it fits the nature of a human being best. As Charlotte Mason said, "Children narrate by nature."[36] In saying this, she was reflecting the Aristotelian tradition, adopted by the Judeo-Christian west, that human nature has some fixed qualities that make some educational or cultural practices better or worse.[37]

For instance, human beings naturally have a capacity for reasoning, so training them in principles of logic and right reason fits their nature. In the same way, human beings can sing and dance and wrestle and run, and these skills can be honed and trained in an ideal manner according to the nature of our human capacities. When that nature is correctly understood and practices are optimally suited to it, training can produce the opera singer who fills the theater hall with his voice, or the ballet dancer leaping and spinning with grace, balance, and poise, or the professional wrestler or four-minute miler.

Narration is in a human being's nature and only requires the right training to bring it to maturity. But perhaps my analogies have led us astray because people do not all dance or sing or wrestle or run with any regularity these days. Charlotte Mason claims that narration is more like our first example of reasoning since it is native to every child's mind:

> Narrating is an art, like poetry-making or painting, because it is there, in every child's mind, waiting to be discovered, and is not the result of any process of disciplinary education. A creative fiat calls it forth. "Let him narrate"; and the child narrates, fluently, copiously, in ordered sequence, with fit and graphic details, with a just choice of words, without verbosity or tautology, so soon as he can speak with ease.[38]

---

36. This is the subheading given to Chapter Nine "The Art of Narration," of part V of Mason's *Home Education* 154.

37. She is thus drawing from the tradition of natural law in moral philosophy, as applied to education specifically; see Kevin Clark and Ravi Jain's cogent discussion of its importance for a recovery of the liberal arts tradition in *The Liberal Arts Tradition: A Philosophy of Christian Classical Education*, 2nd ed. (Classical Academic Press, 2019), 163ff. Camp Hill, PA.

38. Ibid.

We might quibble with Mason here by pointing out that poetry-writing and painting are hardly the normal attainments of every child. But she was not claiming that training or any "disciplinary process" are unnecessary for attaining these arts, just that the art is there in the mind of the child before the training ever comes along to bring it to fruition.[39] Narrating is natural to human beings just like poetry writing or painting, singing, dancing, or running. They are natural endowments of God. They are part and parcel of human nature.

In fact, when Charlotte Mason refered to the "creative fiat" that calls forth narration, she was alluding to the creation story of Genesis, when God said, "Let there be light!" ("Fiat lux" in the Latin *Vulgate*). In the back of her mind, then, was probably the Christian doctrine of the image of God, a fact that no doubt underlies the capacity of human beings to narrate. We reflect the image of our story-telling God.

Of course, at the foundation of this is the power of language itself. By His powerful Word. God spoke the universe into existence, and by that same Word he orders and sustains it. Human beings made in His image have the capacity for language by nature. As Stratford Caldecott puts it in his book *Beauty in the Word*, "Through language we demonstrate and activate our humanity, and channel the faculties of memory, imagination, and thought."[40] Therefore, narration, conceived most generally as telling what has been heard, is imitative of God's creative, communicative nature.

This is what Charlotte Mason meant by claiming that narration was natural. She went on to note how normal children would narrate expertly without instruction, telling a

---

39. While human beings have a capacity for expert performance in other areas, like chess or opera or running four-minute miles, training is necessary to accomplish it ("disciplinary education"), whereas these three communication arts seem to be naturally human and practiced in every culture and time; we think, for instance, of cave paintings found around the globe as an illustration of this.

40. The full title is *Beauty in the Word: Rethinking the Foundations of Education* (Tacoma, WA: Angelico Press, 2012), 38.

story well, "with fit and graphic details," and so on.

This idea that narration is natural serves as the foundation for three distinct reasons for why we should adopt narration as a teaching practice:

1) It is a natural gift of God for children's education.
2) It follows the classical principle of self-education.
3) It enjoys the support of modern research.

A Natural Gift for Education

First of all, if we understand that the ability to narrate is natural, then we can begin to imagine how it could be put to use for the purposes of education. Charlotte Mason puts it this way:

> This amazing gift with which normal children are born is allowed to lie fallow in their education. Bobbie will come home with a heroic narrative of a fight he has seen between "Duke" and a dog in the street. It is wonderful! He has seen everything, and he tells everything with splendid vigour in the true epic vein; but so ingrained is our contempt for children that we see nothing in this but Bobbie's foolish childish way! Whereas here, if we have eyes to see and grace to build, is the ground-plan of his education.[41]

When we truly understand the power of narration to bear fruit in the mind of a child, it is like a field ready to be harvested. Simply sow the seed, and the student will readily grow in knowledge and ability as surely as proper sun and rain lead to harvest.

Perhaps we've never thought of the excitement and eagerness of a young child's storytelling in this way before. There is

---

41. Mason, *Home Education*, 154–155.

something about the activity of narrating itself that rouses and engages the interest of the storyteller just as much as the listener. The inciting action is necessary, but once their interest is enlivened, the story almost tells itself in the child's imagination.

> Stories are the mind's bread and butter. They are the foundation of everything more complex and elaborate in the intellectual life.

One of Charlotte Mason's most convicting appeals throughout her works is this concern that we not despise or have contempt for little children[42]—a thought which she drew from Jesus' warning in the Gospels: "See that you do not despise one of these little ones ..." (Matt. 18:10 [ESV]).

Her point here was that we modern adults may be tempted to undervalue such a telling as "childish" when in fact we have hit upon one of the most powerful tools for sustaining the child's interest and engagement with his own education.

As Charlotte Mason concludes in this same passage, "Let us take the goods the gods provide."[43] In other words, given that narration engages children's minds and hearts in the acquisition of knowledge in this way, let us make the best use of it we can. We might as well build our educational practices on the foundation of how children *actually are* in their nature as opposed to how we might imagine them to be in our modernist preference for abstraction or analytical dissection.

---

42. See, for instance, Mason, *Home Education*, Part I, sections 2–5, pp. 21ff.
43. Ibid., 155.

The Classical Principle of Self-Education

At this point, classical educators might be wondering how this squares with the principles of the classical tradition and all that we've recovered thanks to Dorothy Sayers, C. S. Lewis, and other luminaries of our reform movement.

This brings us to our second reason for adopting narration: it powerfully embodies the classical principle of self-education, which is the classical tradition's idea that students should be taught how to learn for themselves rather than simply being taught facts. They should be taught how to think, not what to think.

Dorothy Sayers probably expressed this idea most memorably at the end of her 1949 essay on the lost tools of learning. Sayers bemoaned how the teachers "are doing for their pupils the work which the pupils themselves ought to do," and she concludes with a statement summing up the heart of her philosophy: "For the sole true end of education is simply this: to teach men how to learn for themselves; and whatever instruction fails to do this is effort spent in vain."[44]

Classical educators may be surprised to learn that Charlotte Mason anticipated her in this. She is often quoted as saying, "There is no education but self-education," by which she meant that the students must do the work of learning for themselves, rather than be spoon-fed by their teachers.[45]

---

44. The text of Sayers' address is widely available online; as of March 2020, a PDF of the whole text can be accessed at https://www.pccs.org/wp-content/uploads/2016/06/LostToolsOfLearning-DorothySayers.pdf.

45. The full quotation in context Mason, *Towards a Philosophy of Education*, 189. It is as follows:

> One thing at any rate we know with certainty, that no teaching, no information becomes knowledge to any of us until the individual mind has acted upon it, translated it, transformed it, absorbed it, to reappear, like our bodily food, in forms of vitality. Therefore, teaching, talk and tale, however lucid or fascinating, effect nothing until self-activity be set up; that is, self-education is the only possible education; the rest is mere veneer laid on the surface of a child's nature.

In her third volume *School Education*, Charlotte Mason claims that:

> **Children must Labour...** [must get] ideas out of [books]... the labour of thought is what his book must induce in the child. He must generalise, classify, infer, judge, visualise, discriminate, labour in one way or another, with that capable mind of his . . . .[46]

Many times in her works, Charlotte Mason bemoaned the flood of ineffective teacher-talk, the type of textbooks that are as dry as sawdust, and the watered-down books for children that she called "twaddle." In her final volume, she said, "I am jealous for the children; every modern educational movement tends to belittle them intellectually."[47]

But of course, it's not as if the principle of self-education was new to either Sayers or Mason. It's simply a truism of the classical tradition itself and one of its most important principles at that.

This principle of self-education derives from a Christian respect for children as persons made in the image of God rather than as empty receptacles waiting to be filled with a teacher's knowledge, poured down as from on high.

Starting with the Enlightenment and moving into the Modern Era, an assumption emerged which asserted that the best thing we could do for children would be to liberate them from the superstitions of the past by filling

---

46. Cited from *Ambleside Online*: https://www.amblesideonline.org/CM/vol3complete.html#179, accessed February 2020.
47. Mason, *Towards a Philosophy of Education*, 28.

them with the assured results of modern science.[48] As Charlotte Mason said, this tends to belittle children's intellectual nature as actually being capable of perceiving and discerning the truth themselves. It privileges the sound bite of "science" to the stories of our tradition. The ultimate end, of course, of neglecting the principle of self-education is to leave children prey to the propagandist and mass-marketer, as Dorothy Sayers so eloquently portrayed.

But Charlotte Mason attempted to head off where this was going through her focus on the students' own work, their own mental, moral, and emotional growth, likening them not to an inanimate basin to be filled or slate to be written on but to a living, breathing mind to be fed with the best food available and given plenty of exercise and outdoor air.[49]

In essence, we could say that students need to be fed on the proper mind-food of knowledge, conveyed in the form of well-written books on every subject and then exercised through practice of narration and other "mental gymnastics."

The practice of narration is the most basic and fundamental way to ensure that the students themselves are doing the work of

48. C. S. Lewis, *The Abolition of Man* (New York: HarperCollins, 2001); 13–14. Tackling the substructure of this problematic development was one of the main purposes of this work which he expresses very charitably:
> I think Gaius and Titius may have honestly misunderstood the pressing educational need of the moment. They see the world around them swayed by emotional propaganda—they have learned from tradition that youth is sentimental—and they conclude that the best thing they can do is to fortify the minds of young people against emotion. My own experience as a teacher tells an opposite tale. For every one pupil who needs to be guarded from a weak excess of sensibility there are three who need to be awakened from the slumber of cold vulgarity. The task of the modern educator is not to cut down jungles but to irrigate deserts. The right defence against false sentiments is to inculcate just sentiments. By starving the sensibility of our pupils we only make them easier prey to the propagandist when he comes.

49. Mason, *Towards a Philosophy of Education*, 26–27:
> The body lives by air, grows on food, demands rest, flourishes on a diet wisely various. So, of the mind,—(by which I mean the entire spiritual nature, all that which is not body),—it breathes in air, calls for both activity and rest and flourishes on a wisely varied dietary.

learning, of assimilating the rich content they have been exposed to by their books and teachers. It adopts the humble stance of imitation rather than the critical stance of debunking.[50] It requires the student to listen and understand before he criticizes and judges. All too often the so-called "critical thinking" of modern educators amounts to indoctrination into their own political ideology.

Instead, the goal that inspired Dorothy Sayers' recovery and application of the trivium was to get students working, thinking, and chewing on the matter of knowledge through the arts of grammar, logic, and rhetoric. In a way that I will describe in more detail later (see Chapter Five), the practice of narration is a core element of all three arts of the trivium. The art of telling is the more basic and fundamental human capacity on which a child's development in the other liberal arts should be based.

> To summarize, we should adopt the practice of narration because it befits a child's nature, provides a powerful ground plan for his education, and perfectly embodies the classical principle of self-education.

The Support of Modern Research

Lastly, narration also enjoys the support of modern research in cognitive psychology and learning science.

Of course, even appealing to modern research might be a controversial move among classical educators. After all, doesn't our movement exist precisely to challenge the hostile takeover

---

50. As such, narration coincides with what has sometimes been called the mimetic mode of the classical tradition as opposed to the didactic mode. However, in a way, it fuses mimetic and didactic into a single learning process in which the teacher presents content to be learned (didactic), and the student then imitates that content (mimetic). For more on this distinction see the CiRCE Institute webpage describing classical education: https://www.circeinstitute.org/resources-what-classical-education/how-teach-classically.

of the "assured results of modern science," as mentioned above? Perhaps we need to remember that it is just as fallacious to accept the ancient unthinkingly as it is to accept the modern because it's modern. The timing of an idea's birth is no assurance of its truth.

We need to beware the echo chamber of classical educators that accepts any idea, no matter its merits, as long as it can appeal to ancient authority.

The thoughtful synthesis of the classical tradition and modern research would not have been a stumbling block to Charlotte Mason. She saw her goal as "to bring common thought on the subject of education to the level of scientific research" by fusing the wisdom of what we call the classical tradition with "some half-dozen physiological and psychological truths" into an organic unity founded on the core principles of Christianity.[51] So much for my defense of citing the support of modern research.

In 2018, I began listening to the Learning Scientists' podcast, which was started by two researchers devoted to popularizing the key empirically verified findings of what strategies actually work to improve learning. The gold standard, what they call the single most important activity to engage in, is what's called **retrieval practice**.[52]

It's exactly what it sounds like—practicing retrieving from memory what the student previously read or heard. It's hard, it's painful, and it reveals how much you don't know that you thought you did. In a way, it's a broader name for narration. The classic example given for retrieval practice is to close your science book, get out a blank sheet of paper, and write down whatever you can recall on a topic from your pure brain.

---

51. Cholmondeley, *The Story of Charlotte Mason*, 17, quoting from Charlotte Mason's address at the first meeting of the Parents' Educational Union in 1887.
52. See www.learningscientists.org especially episode two, "Retrieval Practice."

One of the things these researchers stress is that this is one of the key ways that durable learning—learning that lasts for the long-term—happens. Retrieval practice is not just what you do in studying for a test, though it is the most effective way to do that. It is the process of learning *itself* because it requires your brain to re-access the neural networks that were originally lit up as you were attending to that material. In so doing, the memory of those mental models is encoded in such a way that you can reliably re-access them later. This finding is not controversial but enjoys broad support and multiple attestation among researchers.[53] It's also been recognized in some form or another throughout the classical tradition.

The authors of *Make It Stick: The Science of Successful Learning*, two cognitive psychologists and a novelist, describe it this way:

> The power of retrieval as a learning tool is known among psychologists as the testing effect. In its most common form testing is used to measure learning and assign grades in school, but we've long known that the act of retrieving knowledge from memory has the effect of making that knowledge easier to retrieve in the future. In his essay on memory, Aristotle wrote, "exercise in repeatedly recalling a thing strengthens the memory." Francis Bacon wrote about this phenomenon, as did the psychologist William

---

53. In addition to the citations below from *Make It Stick,* we might note that of the twelve "research-informed strategies" recommended by Glenn Whitman and Ian Kelleher in *Neuroteach: Brain Science and the Future of Education,* numbers two and four directly draw from the research on retrieval practice (Lanham, MA: Rowman and Littlefield, 2016), 27: "Students should be given more frequent, formative, low-stakes assessments of learning," and "Students need to know that the pervasive way they choose to study is actually hurting their ability to learn for the long term and that self-testing is much more effective than reading one's notes."

James. Today we know from empirical research that practicing retrieval makes learning stick far better than reexposure to the original material does. This is the testing effect, also known as the retrieval practice effect.[54]

The studies that have demonstrated this have not, of course, used the practice of narration that we propose here. But they have demonstrated a few propositions that would seem to indicate that narration is one of the most effective ways to utilize the testing effect or retrieval practice.

Here are **a few key findings** as explained in *Make It Stick*:

- "Tests that require the learner to supply the answer, like an essay or short-answer test, or simply practice with flashcards, appear to be more effective than simple recognition tests like multiple choice or true/false tests."[55]
- "While any kind of retrieval practice generally benefits learning, the implication seems to be that where more cognitive effort is required for retrieval, greater retention results."[56]
- "In fact, research indicates that testing, compared to rereading, can facilitate better transfer of knowledge to new contexts and problems, and that it improves one's ability to retain and retrieve material that is related but not tested."[57]
- "After an initial test, *delaying subsequent retrieval practice* is more potent for reinforcing retention than immediate practice, because delayed retrieval requires more effort."[58]

---

54. Peter Brown, Henry Roediger III and Mark McDaniel, *Make It Stick: The Science of Successful* (Cambridge, MA: Belknap, 2014), 23. In the first chapter, the authors explain their method by saying, "We have distilled the findings of a large body of such [empirical] studies that have stood up under review by the scientific community before being published in professional journals" (9).
55. Ibid., 40–41.
56. Ibid., 41.
57. Ibid., 41–42.
58. Ibid., 43.

- "While cramming can produce better results on an immediate exam, the advantage quickly fades because there is much more forgetting after rereading than after retrieval practice. The benefits of retrieval practice are *long-term*."[59]
- "Giving students *corrective feedback* after tests keeps them from incorrectly retaining the material they have misunderstood and produces better learning of the correct answers."[60]

The practice of narration stands on the side of optimal learning in all these findings. Narration calls on the students to supply the answer in a comprehensive way and therefore requires more cognitive effort, leading to better retention. Narration as a practice is opposed to rereading material, studying up, or cramming for tests. As Charlotte Mason stressed, "A single reading is a condition insisted upon because a naturally desultory habit of mind leads us all to put off the effort of attention as long as a second or third chance of coping with our subject is to be hoped for."[61] The immediacy of retrieval practice after this single reading inspires in students full attention the first time. Also, because of the "initial test" of narration, retention is ensured at a high level even if the material is only recalled again sometime later, whether for a later test or a review discussion. Below I will recommend how to ensure that students receive corrective feedback after the narration such that the class learns the content better.

So how do we begin practicing narration in our classical classrooms?

> The practice of narration is a natural gift for our students' education. It accords with their nature as created in the image of our speaking, story-telling God. It embodies the classical principle of self-education by requiring students' minds to do the work of learning themselves. And it enjoys the support of modern research about retrieval practice or the testing effect.

---

60. Ibid.
61. Mason, *Towards a Philosophy of Education*, 132.

Chapter Three

....

KEY STEPS TO IMPLEMENTATION

I have taken so much time discussing the reasons for adopting narration as a practice because, in one sense, the most important strategy for successfully implementing narration is a belief that it works. If a teacher or school administrator fully believes in the effectiveness of narration, they will push through the inevitable hiccups along the road to its successful implementation. Narration breaks many of our modern assumptions about what goes on in a normal classroom. Therefore, a leap of faith is necessary for putting it into practice.

I hope that my explanation of the reasons for narration—how narration accords with a Christian view of children and their nature, how it embodies the classical principle of self-education, and how it enjoys the support of modern research—has given you the confidence to give it a try. As the book of Ecclesiastes says, "A threefold cord is not quickly broken" (Eccl. 4:12 [ESV]). In the same way, where a Christian worldview, the classical tradition, and modern research agree, we are very likely to be on firm ground in our educational practices and can proceed with confidence.

Narration as a practice is simple and flexible, so, even if you left off reading at this point to try it for yourself in whatever way made most sense to you, you would likely find a way to implement it well with even just a moderate degree of perseverance and ingenuity.

However, with more than a decade of experience practicing narration with real students in the classroom, I have many tips and suggestions that may ease your path to implementation and make the practice even more successful than my early attempts were.

These steps include rolling out the practice to your students, setting up a process for how to ask students to narrate, getting additions and corrections from other students, and allowing time for students to develop in their ability to narrate.

The Rollout

So how do you begin implementing narration in your own classical classroom? The first step is to roll out the new practice to your students.[62]

This is simply a function of good leadership and good communication. If you were coaching a soccer team and wanted to begin implementing a new drill, you'd want to take the time to describe the new drill, give some background on its purpose, and explain your goals for the new drill, especially if it were a drill that you intended to use at every practice. If you simply gave them a few quick instructions and set them going, it's possible everything would go okay, but you'd be tempting fate. It's much more likely that the second or third time you used the drill, your players would start complaining, saying things like, "Not this drill again!" or "I don't like

---

62. I owe the terminology of "roll out" to Doug Lemov's *Teach Like a Champion: 62 Techniques That Put Students on the Path to College* (Jossey-Bass: San Francisco, 2015), 365ff.

that drill, why can't we do the other one we always used to?"

Whenever teachers implement a major change in classroom procedure, best practice calls for a rollout, i.e., a little speech explaining the nature of the change, reasons behind it, and what it should look like—potentially even some trial practice of the new procedure.[63] This gives students the opportunity to know what to expect, grapple ahead of time with the implications of the change, and get on board with your reasoning behind it. As the leader of your classroom, you're much less likely to encounter major resistance if you enact major changes only after a good roll out.

Disciplining yourself to prepare a rollout speech also ensures that you craft your instructions for how to do narration thoughtfully. This increases the likelihood that you will communicate what you are looking for as clearly as possible.

A good rollout of the practice of narration should include these four elements:

1. An explanation of what narration is and what it is not.
For example, I strongly encourage talking through the difference between narration and summary: narrations tell as much detail as possible, while summaries try to highlight only the main points. Other than that, the chapters above should provide you with some ideas to boil down for them.

2. A description of how narration will help them learn.
While it might be tempting to talk about Charlotte Mason or

---

63. Lemov calls this teaching practice "Strategic Investment: From Procedure to Routine" (*Teach Like a Champion*, 49), describing it this way: "Turn procedures into routines by rehearsing and reinforcing until excellence becomes habitual. Routinizing a key procedure requires clear expectations, consistency, and most important, patience" (365). This key pedagogical insight coheres well with Charlotte Mason's emphasis on the importance of habits as the "railways of life" and education as a discipline.

the classical tradition, since these sources are not necessarily embraced by all our students as authoritative, I have found that describing briefly how memory formation works in our brains is the most convincing. In the chapter on retrieval practice, the authors of *Make It Stick* describe a number of specific studies that have proven its effectiveness. One of these may resonate with your students.[64]

3. What your expectations are for them.

It's best to be clear that you expect them to attend as best they can to the passage as it's read (or to whatever other form the content takes: painting, lecture, demonstration, etc.) and that they should do their very best to tell everything they can remember but also that there is no expectation that they will remember everything perfectly. You want to raise the expectation of focus but simultaneously deflate any performance anxiety that some may feel. We're looking for a full effort, not perfectionism.

4. Some tips and tricks for how to get better at narrating.

Encourage your students by explaining that narrating is valuable for learning content right now, but it's also something they can get better and better at. A couple of tips include imagining or trying to picture what's happening in

---

64. See Brown et al., *Make It Stick*, 30ff. I recommend, in particular, the following:

The first large-scale investigation was published in 1917. Children in grades 3, 5, 6, and 8 studied brief biographies from *Who's Who in America*. Some of them were directed to spend varying lengths of the study time looking up from the material and silently reciting to themselves what it contained. Those who did not do so simply continued to reread the material. At the end of the period, all the children were asked to write down what they could remember. The recall test was repeated three to four hours later. All the groups who had engaged in the recitation showed better retention than those who had not done so but had merely continued to review the material. The best results were from those spending about 60 percent of the study time in recitation. (30)

your mind's eye, rather than focusing on individual words and not worrying about trying to memorize the whole passage, but simply starting at the beginning and asking yourself, "What's next?"

The final suggestion I would give for the rollout is to adopt a tone of confidence and excitement. The emotional mood of a teacher's expression can have a remarkable influence on the perceptions of students. Avoid accidentally suggesting that narration is a burdensome activity. It is fine and even advisable to prepare students for the fact that narration will not necessarily be easy, but you should express at the same time that it is well worth the effort and that the goal is for them to learn as much as possible. You as a teacher are bound to help them learn as well as they possibly can, and narration will help them in that process. You might even encourage students to give their narrations a dramatic flair. Energy and interest are good signs, and the more they can be cultivated early on the better.

How to Ask Your Students to Narrate

A specific method for asking students to narrate might seem like a non-issue to some, but it can have an outsized effect on its long-term effectiveness.

I can imagine that some teachers, especially at the beginning, might be inclined to ask for volunteers to narrate. This can be tempting as a way to ease the transition to narrating. However, it will instead prolong the transition by creating the impression that narration is optional. Some students may try to avoid narrating as long as possible, and, assuming you have more than a few students in the class, they may very well be successful. In the meantime, they may develop more of a performance anxiety or fear around the practice, because their avoidance of it has caused it to loom large in their imagination.

It's also true in general that if some students feel that they can avoid a learning activity by opting out, a suboptimal learning environment is the inevitable result. High academic expectations can only be established if 100 percent of your students know that they are accountable for doing the work of learning 100 percent of the time. This is why it's crucial to use cold calling as your primary method of asking your students to narrate.[65]

Cold calling is when the teacher calls on students directly, ensuring that all students are held accountable all the time. Adopting a tactic to include the whole class and randomizing your choice is helpful as well. Since there are a limited number of opportunities for students to narrate aloud throughout any given school day, a teacher should attempt to ensure that every student is called on to narrate in some form at least once each day.

NOTA BENE For the terminology of "cold calling" as well as other concepts mentioned here, like 100 percent participation, I am reliant on Doug Lemov's *Teach Like a Champion*. There are few modern books on teaching that I would recommend more than *Teach Like a Champion* for its taxonomy of teaching practices.

Originating from the charter school movement and Lemov's analysis of what successful teachers in some of the most underperforming areas did differently, *TLaC 2.0* embodies many of the principles of traditional or classical education in a creative way that suited its unique context.

A key classical principle they employ includes the idea that no student should be able to "opt out" of the work of learning. Instead, students should all be held accountable to participate, even if that just means listening to a fellow classmate's answer and repeating it.

65. See Lemov, *Teach Like a Champion*, "Technique 11: No Opt Out," 90–99; "Technique 33: Cold Call," 249–261; and for the idea of 100 percent, Chapter Two on High Behavioral Expectations, 387.

Also, the format in which students answer questions matters, and they should be held to as high a standard of correctness as possible rather than being given indiscriminate praise at every attempt. The reward for a right answer should be follow-up questions that take the discussion further. In other words, learning more and harder things is the natural reward for successful learning.[66]

One of my early inventions for implementing cold calling well is what I call the *Cards of Destiny*. They are simply a set of laminated cards with each student's name on the back. When coming to any opportunity for a student to narrate content in class, the student is chosen randomly by a flip of the card. Destiny decides the next narrator! If you use this tactic often for calling on students to read, answer questions, or engage in other normal classroom activities, it's even more effective because it allows the practice of narration to blend in with everything else that goes on in the classroom.

Besides the obvious goal of ensuring that you don't call on the same set of students too many times to the neglect of other students, there are some added benefits to using randomized cards. First, some students occasionally respond to cold calling by taking it personally, as if you were singling them out from the class. With the Cards of Destiny in hand, you can explain to students that everyone is expected to participate, and you are using the cards to decide so that everyone gets called on equally. This will help some students who might otherwise experience performance anxiety with narrating overcome it by the clear and open acknowledgement of fairness and the fact that everyone else is clearly going along with the system.

---

66. See ibid., "Technique 12: Right Is Right," 100–107; "Technique 13: Stretch It," 108–115; "Technique 14: Format Matters," 116–121.

It is perhaps worth pausing to note at this point that the problem of performance anxiety is a legitimate one that students face. When the brain is in a state of high anxiety or fear, the higher order cognitive functions operating out of the frontal lobes are largely shut down. The fight or flight response has taken over at this point and intellectual heavy lifting is not going to be possible until the student recovers emotionally.[67] We have all experienced the memory blank that sometimes occurs from being put on the spot publicly in a way we're not used to. This is natural and is best overcome through familiarity with the requirement and lowering the stakes.

At the same time, holding out for a response and keeping accountability present are important for the student's long-term development. A helpful tactic with a student who is clearly drawing a blank because of fear/anxiety is to remain with the student through eye-contact, expressing your willingness to wait patiently and exuding a calm, contented emotional presence with them through that challenging moment. If they cannot tell anything even after pushing past the fear moment, then another student can be called on and you can tell this student before the next reading that you will call on them after, so they have the chance to prepare themselves emotionally.

A second benefit of the Cards of Destiny is that, as teachers, we can fall into the trap of calling on certain students too often, perhaps because we see them engaging in some less than fully attentive behavior. In such cases, we tend to call on them either deliberately, as a sort of gotcha to get the student to realize the need to attend, or subconsciously because that student has caught our attention and his or her name happens to be at the front of our mind. There are already so many things for us to

---

67. This idea also makes the list of Whitman and Kelleher's top twelve research-informed strategies, emphasizing in particular students' own awareness of this principle: "Students need to love their limbic system and recognize the impact stress, fear, and fatigue have on the higher-order thinking and memory parts of their brain" (*Neuroteach*, 27). In the chapter end note eight they cite numerous studies to this effect. Also, see their discussion of the amygdala specifically: "Too much stress impedes learning because the amygdala sends incoming information from your senses to the primordially hardwired reactive "fight, flight, freeze" part of the brain, rather than the reflective part of the brain, the prefrontal cortex ..." (35).

focus on in the classroom as teachers that it is a helpful weight off the mind to assign the choice of who next to a random system. Sometimes, in spite of our best efforts and intentions, students can have legitimate reasons for supposing that we are "picking on them" and systems like this can help to avoid that.

Third, using cards also saves time that could have otherwise been wasted in different methods of choosing the next narrator. Again, most teachers are paying attention to a lot of different moving parts in the classroom and may not always be aware of how long a pause occurs as they wait for volunteers. After such a pause, they finally call on a student who opts out, claiming he forgot. Next, they take a volunteer, who happens to be the same student who narrated last time, which they only realize after another moment. They then finish up by calling on a compliant student, because there's no way the teacher wants to risk calling on a harder student at this point. Throughout all this, the clock has been ticking as precious seconds for learning pass by.

If that sounds far-fetched, then you haven't observed in many classrooms! The path of least resistance often privileges the students who need accountability the least.

The quick and effective method of randomized cards helps create the atmosphere of full accountability while avoiding any appearance of injustice as well as any actual arbitrary choice on the part of the teacher. Cold calling in this manner can

An improvement on the basic set of cards with students' names is the double set. Some of my fellow teachers noticed that with one set of cards, students over time developed te tendency to sit back on their laurels after they were called on. They assumed, correctly that since they had just been called on to arrate, it would be quite some time before the cards got around to them again. Now we all have a double set that we shuffle regularly, meaning that each student has a second card in there that could come up any time. There should be no tme in the school day that students don't feel a sense of accountability to learn whatever new knowledge is being presented to them.

be a powerful tool for normalizing the practice of narration quickly in your classroom and avoiding any possible backlash that might have otherwise resulted.

All that I have said so far applies primarily to the first and most basic method of narrating: the spoken narration of one student before the class. This is the essential baseline method of narrating that you should focus on first in your implementation process. Once your students are comfortable with it, then other variations can be used that each have their trade-offs.

Varieties of Narration

String Narration

String narration is the most basic development of oral narration. Instead of having only one student tell back the passage, you call on multiple students to narrate from where the previous student left off. Each student strings together the narration in succession. In this way, after reading a passage out of a literature book, say, you could involve three or four students in the process of narrating. This improves the participation ratio of students actively engaged and enables the teacher to hold every student accountable for following along as the other students narrate since they will need to be ready to jump in and continue the collective narration at any point.[68] String narration involves the added complexity of requiring the teacher to interrupt students mid-stream and ask other students to continue where they left off. Because of this, it should only be implemented after students have achieved some

---

68. Participation ratio is also a concept borrowed from Lemov, *Teach Like a Champion*, 234. In this case, because of narration, participation ratio and think ratio roughly coincide since narration is naturally rigorous.

fluency with single-student oral narration.[69] It also works best with longer passages, ideally from literary texts like a history book or a novel.

The best way to interrupt a student is to say their name, thank them, and then ask the next student to pick up where they left off. This allows you to quickly acknowledge the work of the student and keep the flow going as soon as possible.

To get more from students with a shorter passage it is ideal to move to the next step of taking additions and corrections (see next chapter). For older students who may have been assigned to read a chapter or two of such a text at home, string narration can be the ideal way to begin a class focused on that reading.

Partner or Group Narration

A second variety of oral narration is to assign students to partners or groups and have a system for calling on one student to narrate to the other(s). With table partners, for instance, the teacher can easily instruct the person on the left to tell back to the person on the right, or vice versa. Then the other can be asked to make additions and corrections at the end (see next section for details on this step). Groups could be assigned colors or some other organizing system to make the teacher's instructions quick and clear.

Like string narration, the benefit of partner or group narration is that more students are given the chance to narrate. While simply hearing another student narrate mimics the effect of

---

69. String narration is one of the first types of narration suggested by Charlotte Mason in the context of a parent or governess as educator, as illustrated by *Home Education*, 156: "Then, she may read two or three pages, enough to include an episode; after that, let her call upon the children to narrate,—in turns, if there be several of them."

narrating oneself, since the student's mind is all the while comparing his or her own memories and checking them against what is told by the other student, it is still true that the more students narrate the better. Using partner narration raises the participation ratio up to 50 percent—a significant increase that can lead to very real improvements in student learning.

The danger with partner or group narration is the possibility of diminishing quality of narrations. Some students and groups may use the plausible anonymity of a large group of students narrating across the room to opt out of a full effort. Without you and everyone else listening in all the time, there is less pressure to perform well, and the inertia of laziness or half-effort can kick in.

This danger can be minimized in a few different ways. First, teachers should generally wait to implement partner narration until after single-student narration has been established and is being practiced with a good degree of regularity and success. If students are still weak at narrating or are pushing back against the practice, partner narration will be unlikely to solve these problems and will possibly make them worse.

Second, teachers should always actively circulate the room during partner narration, listening closely for the quality of student's narrations and periodically calling out a correction or encouragement to full effort. Third, when setting up partner or group narration, you should encourage students to hold one another accountable. The right type of peer accountability can enforce a culture of effort and learning better than the strictest punishments. It can be refreshing to hear one student gently chastising her partner for not telling back right away or as fully as she knows he can. There are still times when I see that partner narration is diminishing in quality and a fresh encouragement or different approach needs to be employed.

In this, as in so many other things, it's helpful to be clear up front about proper expectations for partner or group narrations. Ask the students themselves to come up with a list of things to remember that will make them learn best. Students thrive on the chance to set the bar for themselves. Lastly, partner or group narration can be noisy, and it may be useful to prepare students with an encouragement to focus only on what they are saying to their partner and not on the narrations in any other groups.

Written Narration

Last but certainly not least is the method of asking students to write out their narration in a notebook or on loose leaf paper. This method of narration boasts the highest possible participation percentage of 100 percent. Every student works on producing their own composition, imitating to the best of their ability the style, substance, and structure of the original material.

Written narration relies on a student's ability to write with at least a moderate level of fluency. Of course, it is also a powerful tool for helping students develop in their fluency as writers. By fluency, I mean the ability to get into the flow of writing, rather than be constantly stopping and starting because of lack of familiarity with letter formation, spelling, or other writing conventions.

A few supports can be put in place to help students get into the flow and progress with written narration.[70] First, the teacher can give a sort of rudimentary outline on the board indicating the major items to hit. Since the students are facing the extra challenge of writing, which requires them to slow down from their natural speed of thought, this scaffolding can help them get back on track quickly and prevent unnecessary slow-downs due to a student getting distracted and forgetting what was next.

---

70. Readers who are interested in a fuller treatment of written narration from the perspective of home education are referred to Karen Glass' *Know and Tell*, Chapter Five "Developing Written Narration" (65–87).

Second, the teacher should consider writing tough words and proper nouns on the board. These can operate both as memory cues and as models of the proper spelling. Often the passage will introduce some new vocabulary, names, and places; the added complexity of trying to spell correctly from memory might lead some students to avoid those important words when they would enrich their narrations and lead to more in-depth learning. Reducing the friction by writing them on the board can be effective and, for more advanced students, can represent a goal of getting all the important words and proper nouns into their narration.

In general, students should be encouraged to ask the teacher for the spelling of any word they don't know. Spelling tests are the proper time for students to try to reproduce the spelling of words from memory because there they have had the benefit of studying or memorizing the specific words and rules that apply. Written narrations will help develop students' spelling knowledge and instincts best if they have recourse to a teacher, parent, or dictionary to write the word down correctly the first time. Writing a word incorrectly tends to cement the incorrect spelling in the memory even if it is corrected later.[71] Encouraging students to ask for help with spelling also helps them build awareness of when they do and when they do not know how to spell a word. And with spelling, self-awareness can be half the battle.

Third, students who finish early with narrations that are not as full as they might be should be encouraged to read back over their material and bullet point or make footnotes of details that they could add to make it better. This challenges all students to use their

---

71. For this reason, I am inclined to nuance advice that is sometimes given that "written narration is not evaluated for spelling and grammar, but for content alone" (Cooper, *When Children Love to Learn*, 130). This may be ideal for emerging writers, but should not be applied after the applicable spelling and grammar rules should have been mastered. Written narration should, whenever possible, be made an opportunity to practice correct spelling and grammar, and unnecessary mistakes should be avoided.

time well for learning. In rare cases, a very weak student could be required to read the passage again silently, before closing the book and adding another paragraph or two, even if it is out of order. In principle, passages should not be reread to encourage focused attention during the first exposure, but individual students also need to be held accountable for learning. With some students, the natural consequence of rereading and then writing more will disincentivize a lack of effort. Alternately, the second try might serve as a scaffold to the student with truly low reading comprehension.

For less time-intensive or polished written narrations, each student could be called on to use a personal white board to bullet point their narration. This could be followed up by reporting to the class, a partner, or a group. Such a practice can be ideal for quick reviews of previous content at the start of a new class or for class periods in which you anticipate a response activity taking a longer amount of time.

As students grow in fluency with written narrations, it may become desirable to use them as assessments, whether formative or summative, on the students' mastery of content in various subjects. In such a case, a written narration can be graded according to a rubric that focuses on different aspects of content, like use of the author's language, the proper sequence of the story, or the details or facts employed.[72] Whatever system a teacher or school devises, it is important to recognize the complex nature of the task of narration and not overly penalize students who are on a journey of developing fluency and cannot reasonably be expected to demonstrate mastery yet.

Narration is about investing in students' learning through building a complex skill over time. Overly quantifying the process is unlikely to help and may cause harm. In early stages of implementation, if grades must be assigned, I would recommend grading based on completion or effort rather than a precise accounting or comparison

---

72. Karen Glass's chart, "Evaluating Narrations," is also a helpful resource on this topic (*Know and Tell*, 59).

of details. Long form narration prompts can be used in summative exams and these should be graded in the same subjective format that essay responses normally receive.[73]

Additions and Corrections

In Chapter One while discussing the reasons for narration, I mentioned the importance of providing students with feedback during retrieval practice in order to correct and improve their knowledge. An important but easily overlooked part of practicing narration is taking additions and corrections from students after the narration is complete.

Charlotte Mason recommends against teasing students with corrections or questions during their narrations because of how it breaks up their train of thought.[74] Imagine trying to express yourself fully and at any length on material you were just exposed to, only to have someone interrupting you all along the way with questions about specific details like names or places.

This can be tempting for the teacher because of a misplaced concern for the truth and making sure students know "the right answer." Especially at the beginning, students may not have caught every detail, and they may even have misunderstood the passage in some serious way. Teachers should resist the urge to correct students on the spot in the middle of their narration. With the practice of narration, we are playing the long game on students' development, trusting that, with time and practice and the steady influx of knowledge that narration brings, students will grasp more and more of the new content they are exposed to and comprehend it better and better.

Besides the obvious negative of interrupting the student,

---

73. The prompt should be open in format but indicate a clear starting and ending point in a story or a clear designation of a topic in a non-narrative subject, like, "Tell back all you can about the bodily structure, life cycle and habitat of bees. You may use a figure or drawing if you wish, but make sure to explain it fully."

74. E.g., Mason, *Home Education*, 156: "It is not wise to tease them with corrections; they may begin with an endless chain of "ands," but they soon leave this off, and their narrations become good enough in style and composition to be put in a 'print book'!"

prompting with questions and giving corrections *during* the narration can have the side effect of making your students too reliant on you as the teacher. Also, it prevents them from developing the habit of patiently listening to someone before making an addition or correction once they have finished. If there's a conversational virtue our culture desperately needs, it's the ability to listen to another person patiently and attentively and still express one's own view afterward. The classical classroom should be a training ground for this habit.

The time for additions and corrections is after the narrator has finished. It's crucial for the teacher to establish the habit of asking for additions or corrections from other students every time, not just when the narration is obviously lacking or incorrect. If you just ask for additions or corrections after weak narrations, you are manifesting a tell that removes the initiative from the students. Think of the inexperienced card player who gives away a bluff by scratching his ear every time.

In line with the classical principle of self-education, we want the students to do the work of learning whenever possible. If a student can express the addition or correction without any prompting from you, that much more cognitive lifting has been offloaded onto the students, and they are developing the intellectual habits of accuracy and thoroughness in their speech.

It is also advisable to ask for additions and corrections in a way that assumes that students will have something to add or correct. While it may seem subtle, there can be an outsized difference that accrues from asking, "What can we add or correct?" rather than, "Are there any additions or corrections?" In the vast majority of cases, there are things to add or correct in the child's narration. So our question should assume as much.

The more that students can be enculturated into the expectation that adding and correcting are helpful and important activities, the better. A lengthy pause after asking, even if there are no immediate volunteers, helps to establish this as your expectation.

At the beginning, and in cases where something important was missed or expressed incorrectly, you as the teacher may want to offer your own addition or correction. This should only need to be used sparingly, but it can also send a powerful implicit message to your class that you care about the content and are invested in it as well.

What we're aiming for is a positive upward spiral in students' attention, comprehension, and learning. The practices outlined here—including the single exposure to content, cold calling on students directly, not allowing students to hide or opt out, expecting all to attend well enough to narrate aloud in detail, followed by the additions and corrections of fellow students— are meant to operate together to build a culture-shaping learning environment. Students are expected to attend and assimilate, to know and tell the new content with a full effort every lesson.

> The high expectations reinforced in every stage and at every level of the process create a powerful synergy that will foster deep learning.

NOTA BENE Of course, it is possible that in any particular lesson, you may choose to skip the additions and corrections step after a single-student narration. You may be behind in your plans for the day and trying to race on to the next section or activity. This is all well and good. However, I would encourage you not to make this a regular practice, especially in early stages of implementation. The additions and corrections step has tremendous value for normalizing the expectation that students pay close attention to each others' narrations, with a view to accuracy and fullness.

In most classrooms and with most subjects there will be several students who are more than eager (and able) to make additions and corrections to others' narrations and giving them an opportunity to do so acts as a spur to the whole class. When some students speak confidently and eagerly about the content, the whole class listens, and love for learning in that area can become contagious. The knowledge that other students are judging their narration in this fashion prods each individual student toward greater effort.

Allow Time for Students to Develop

Given what I wrote about the high expectations of the whole narration process, the teacher just beginning implementation should be patient. As an experienced practitioner of narration at a school claiming remarkable results daily, I can assure you that it works. But students will need time to adjust to these high expectations.

The level of focused attention required for narration is considerable. If you are a teacher at a school that has not implemented narration on a larger scale, you may feel yourself going against the grain somewhat. Beware of too-high expectations in the short term. At my school, all our teachers are regularly expected to read and narrate themselves in faculty training. Because of this, we all know firsthand what we are expecting of our students. Some understanding at the challenge of the transition is in order at the same time as a steady determination that students can and should rise to the challenge with time.

Students new to a school like ours, where narration is a standard teaching practice across subjects and grade levels, can be expected to transition in and develop into more fluent narrators within a couple months, depending on grade level and any particular struggles the child may face. Some students can narrate fairly well from their first day!

The point is that implementing narration is not something you try on a Monday, assess on the Wednesday, and give up on that Friday. Narration is a complex linguistic and intellectual skill. While it is within the mind of every child, you should expect a process of development and commit to the practices that will give it the structure and discipline it needs to grow and finally flourish. The paradoxical key is to set up the expectations that every student can and will narrate and at the same time coax out their growth with grace and ease.

During the transition process, patience is also needed in the various stages of narration itself. When calling on a student to narrate, give them time to gather their thoughts without prompting them. Some teachers are not accustomed to silence and waiting in their classroom. The practice of narration necessitates it. At first, a student may be so shocked that all eyes are on her that it's all she can do to gather her thoughts and make a couple of comments. Establish both your expectation that everyone will narrate and your patience with students who pause to gather their thoughts. Wait patiently and expectantly with a smile on your face. Refuse to make excuses for children when they did not attend or their mind blanks, but do not chastise them, either. Let them know you will call on them again next time so that they can mentally prepare. Be patient and kind but firmly expectant, and the students are sure to get the hang of it with time and practice.

....

CHAPTER FOUR

USING NARRATION IN LESSONS

While the main subject of this book is implementing narration in the classical classroom, the practice of narration assumes a surrounding lesson structure. You might think of narration as a sort of backbone or skeleton on which the flesh and blood of a full-bodied lesson can be built.

Of course, narration can be used for various purposes at many points within a given lesson. Any time there is an occasion for students to retrieve content from memory, they can be called upon to do so. The only difference between narration and structured review led by the teacher's questions is that narration asks that students recall as much as possible about a particular topic. In fact, narration can even be used effectively for rehearsing a teacher's instructions or the steps to follow in an activity or procedure. Any content students have been exposed to that you want them to assimilate or review is worthy of being narrated.

But narration is by its nature a central learning strategy and not just a review strategy. As such, narration can be incorporated into every lesson, and, in order for students to gain facility with it, enough practice is essential.

Teachers who are used to centering their lessons on other types of learning strategies may have a number of feelings at the changes involved in adopting narration. A common one might go something like this: "Is this really all I'm supposed to do? Ask the students to narrate and let them correct themselves? It feels like I'm not teaching anything." Part of this feeling is due to the radical change involved in truly embodying the classical principle of self-education. Although Dorothy Sayers advocated that education should teach children to learn for themselves, still, the assumptions of modern education have so seeped into our expectations, even in our classical schools, that a core practice like narration can be a huge shift. We feel like we should be doing *more teaching*, because modern education has focused too much on the teacher as the source rather than the facilitator of learning.

In contrast to this, Charlotte Mason often talked about how the Holy Spirit is the educator of mankind, referencing Renaissance frescoes like that of the Spanish Chapel in Santa Maria Novella, which depicted a dove descending upon all the captain figures of the liberal arts and sciences.[75] Narration puts the focus on the students having a mind-to-mind interaction with the thoughts of a great author or painter or the truths of mathematics or science.

On the other hand, though, it is important to stress that narration itself isn't everything; in fact, it works best as a practice focused on the students' assimilation of knowledge. It doesn't remove the teacher's responsibility to prepare the students well

---

75. Mason visited Florence in 1893 and "received a deep and living impression of the frescoes on the wall of the Spanish Chapel attached to the Church of Santa Maria Novella. In *Parents and Children*, vol. 2 she devotes a chapter to them, calling it 'The Great Recognition.'" See Chomondeley, *The Story of Charlotte Mason*, 49. They show "the descent of the Holy Spirit upon the mind of men. Within His light are the Apostles and the prophets, and below, centrally enthroned, sits St Thomas Aquinas. Above him float the figures of the seven virtues. In a row at the foot of the picture, beautiful in dignity and alertness, sit the fourteen 'knowledges' or sciences, accompanied by their greatest exponents" (50).

beforehand, faithfully set up the structures for optimal learning, and help the students further digest and apply the new content afterward. Narration is a central piece of a larger puzzle. And only when the teacher has delivered herself of the student's task as the reciter of content can she then focus her attention on other important parts of the lesson. Ultimately, it is a matter of focus.

If you have begun to implement narration, and you are looking for where your skill as a teacher lies with this central practice in place, this chapter is for you. There is much room for the teacher's diligent study, preparation, and skill in execution, even with such a simple and elegant practice like narration at the core of the lesson.

A Lesson Structure for Younger Students

In *Home Education,* Charlotte Mason gave the following suggestions for the short narration lessons of young children (up to nine years old):

> **Method of Lesson**—In every case the reading should be consecutive from a well-chosen book. Before the reading for the day begins, the teacher should talk a little (and get the children to talk) about the last lesson, with a few words about what is to be read, in order that the children may be animated by expectation; but she should beware of explanation and, especially, of forestalling the narrative. Then, she may read two or three pages, enough to include an episode; after that, let her call upon the children to narrate,—in turns, if there be several of them .... The book should always be deeply interesting, and when the narration is over, there should be a little talk in which moral points are brought out, pictures

shown to illustrate the lesson, or diagrams drawn on the blackboard. As soon as children are able to read with ease and fluency, they read their own lesson, either aloud or silently, with a view to narration; but where it is necessary to make omissions, as in the Old Testament narratives and Plutarch's Lives, for example, it is better that the teacher should always read the lesson which is to be narrated.[76]

We can note a few important points from this basic narration lesson structure:

- The lesson begins with **a little talk** that aims to review, prepare, and raise expectation for the new content.

- The reading should be the next passage **from a rich text** ("well-chosen" and "deeply interesting") and can be read aloud by the teacher, aloud by the students ("as soon as children are able to read with ease and fluency"), or silently by the students.

- After the narration, there should be **a second little talk** focused on discussing "moral points," illustrating details through pictures or diagrams, or applying, organizing, or using the new knowledge in some way.

All in all, Charlotte Mason mentions that this short lesson for young children should not take more than fifteen minutes. But the books she recommends for six-to-eight-year-olds are of high caliber indeed: *Robinson Crusoe*, *Pilgrim's Progress*, *Heroes of Asgard*, as well as geography and "sketches from ancient history."[77]

---

76. Mason, *Home Education*, 155–156.
77. Ibid., 155.

A Lesson Structure for Older Students

For older students, she recommends longer lessons and a steadily increasing challenge in content across all subjects until the oldest students at her schools were reading and narrating from, for instance, Sir Francis Bacon's essays and other difficult philosophical and academic material. In her third volume, *School Education*, she discussed the value of narration again, calling it "the simplest way of dealing with a paragraph or chapter" and insisting on a single reading as the best for avoiding the lazy habit of what we call today the in-one-ear-and-out-the-other syndrome.

But then she goes on to enumerate a list of other responses to content:

> **Other Ways of Using Books.**—But this is only one way to use books: others are to enumerate the statements in a given paragraph or chapter; to analyse a chapter, to divide it into paragraphs under proper headings, to tabulate and classify series; to trace cause to consequence and consequence to cause; to discern character and perceive how character and circumstance interact; to get lessons of life and conduct, or the living knowledge which makes for science, out of books; all this is possible for school boys and girls, and until they have begun to use books for themselves in such ways, they can hardly be said to have begun their education.[78]

Note how the opening to this sentence (and paragraph—it is a single-sentence paragraph!) makes it clear that Charlotte Mason does not view narration as the end-all-be-all. She calls it "only one

---

78. *Ambleside Online*: https://www.amblesideonline.org/CM/vol3complete.html#180, accessed February 2020.

way to use books." Thus, despite what some Charlotte Mason enthusiasts claim, it was not, for her, the only proper method of engaging students in the process of learning.[79] Her lesson structure was flexible, relying on narration as the "simplest way" of applying the principle of self-education but also encouraging a variety of what she calls "disciplinary devices" for responding to content.

This makes sense given what we know from modern research on retrieval practice, which encompasses a broader category of responses to knowledge than narration proper. Likewise, the classical tradition embodied the principle of self-education in other ways that nevertheless required the student's minds to do the work of assimilating and thinking through content.

Second, many of these other responses are analytical in nature or involve abstracting ideas out of content rather than simply reproducing the content in a similar format. This might be surprising given what was said above in favor of narration as less analytical and more holistic. However, a paragraph later Mason still expresses concern that such methods could be approached in a way that squelches the heart of a book:

---

79. An example of the view of narration as the only proper method for assimilating text can be illustrated from Maryellen's comments in *When Children Love to Learn*, culminating in a quotation from Mr. Household, an education secretary in the western county of Gloucestershire in the 1920s who was a devoted disciple of Mason's ways (but too willing perhaps to engage in hyperbolic expression of her views), 132:

There is a danger of supplementing the method of narration with general talking and questioning, losing the clarity of a point-by-point argument posited by a writer. . . . If the mind is to be active, it must do the work of attending, reflective thinking, and expression through the work of narration. One cannot omit that part of the lesson where the child puts his mind to the task of retelling through reflective thinking, where he performs the "act of knowing" through verbal or written expression. . . . "[W]e must never forget that without narration the mind will starve; whatever disciplinary exercises we use, they should be in addition to and never instead of narration."

This seems to be precisely against the exact wording of the passage above from Mason's *School Education*. Of course, it is always possible that Mason changed her view, but in that case, the issue would still have had some ambivalence in her thinking.

> These few hints by no means cover the disciplinary
> uses of a good school-book; but let us be careful that
> our disciplinary devices, and our mechanical devices
> to secure and tabulate the substance of knowledge,
> do not come between the children and that which is
> the *soul* of the book, the living thought it contains.[80]

Charlotte Mason puts a premium on a genuine interaction with the heart of a book rather than engaging in analytical exercises as if for their own sake, as some educators of her own day might have been inclined to do. But it is not an all-or-nothing issue for her. Assignments for responding to rich texts are a matter of the teacher's discernment. The skill of the teacher is involved in proper planning and in assigning the work that will best develop their students' knowledge and skills in genuine interaction with quality content.

Charlotte Mason expresses it this way:

> The teacher's part is, in the first place, to see what
> is to be done, to look over the work of the day in
> advance and see what mental discipline, as well as
> what vital knowledge, this and that lesson afford;
> and then to set such questions and such tasks as
> shall give full scope to his pupils' mental activity.[81]

This call to action allows a significant amount of room for the creativity, insight, and skill development of the teacher. At the same time, notice how it maintains a commitment to the principle of self-education; the students are to do the work of learning for themselves. Just as Sayers called for education to be focused on students learning how to learn, Mason is concerned

---

80. *Ambleside Online*: https://www.amblesideonline.org/CM/vol3complete. html#181, accessed February 2020.
81. *Ambleside Online*: https://www.amblesideonline.org/CM/vol3complete. html#180, accessed February 2020.

that teachers "give full scope" to their students' "mental activity."

The goal of a teacher's planning, instruction, and assignments should be to develop her students' minds fully, both by "mental discipline" and with "vital knowledge." She encourages us to avoid the danger of privileging one at the expense of the other.

NOTA BENE In Charlotte Mason's day, the faculty theory of education (or Faculty Psychology) was widespread. The faculty theory held that students should learn Latin, abstract math, and other challenging subjects primarily for the mental discipline involved.[82] The idea was that, even if such subjects were not directly "useful" to their future work, they provided training of certain mental faculties that would be useful. While some classical educators today have embraced the faculty theory as a continuation of the classical tradition, it arose as a defense against early pragmatism and may have conceded too much of the wrong ground. Modern research has demonstrated that such mental faculties do not exist, and subject knowledge and skills in one domain do not readily transfer to other domains.

Of course, intellectual and moral virtues—like accuracy, careful thought, and perseverance—do transfer, but that is something quite different from what the faculty theorists meant and is altogether more clearly attested throughout the classical tradition. Faculty theorists were attempting to defend a particular version of classicism that focused intently on ancient languages and abstract math to the exclusion of the breadth of humane studies as well as more practical-seeming new disciplines, like science, business studies, and economics. I would argue that a more robust vision of the liberal arts and sciences, like that of the Renaissance or classical era itself, would have kept a due focus on all subjects and not narrowly proscribed the canon to Latin and Greek grammar and math.

---

82. A helpful overview of Faculty Psychology can be found at "Faculty Theory and Mental Discipline: A Brief Overview," http://www.eds-resources.com/facultytheory.htm, accessed June, 2020.

The Full Narration Lesson Structure

If we put all the pieces together from these two passages (and other places in Charlotte Mason's works), we come up with a lesson plan with the following possible steps:

1. First Little Talk
2. Reading of a Rich Text
3. Narration
4. Second Little Talk
5. Response

For older students, it seems that the response step, "our disciplinary devices ... to secure and tabulate the substance of knowledge", (see p. 65) could eclipse narration itself and become the whole of the lesson. In Mason's practice, there was also a general trend from reading aloud for younger students to older students silently reading on their own; this shift occurred as students grew in ability and depending on the nature of the text. In the same vein, for younger students, a response of some kind to the text might not be a regular feature in their lessons although in her schools, young children did often respond to their texts in less analytical and more imaginative ways, such as illustrating a scene from one of their literature books.

How often should teachers use narration versus an analytical response with older students? The answer can be illustrated by the idea of a hurdle rate. Doug Lemov applies the economic idea of a hurdle rate or "a rate of return on an investment of her time that she must exceed to make it worthwhile" to the classroom practice of meaningful reading.[83] He imagines the hypothetical possibility of spending all of class time, six to seven hours a day, engaged in the practice of meaningful reading with occasional "summaries and analyses of what they've read." He then poses the question:

---

83. Lemov, *Teach Like a Champion*, 180–181.

> If you could ensure that the reading was of reason-
> able quality, might reading for six or seven hours a
> day, 190 days a year, achieve better outcomes than
> those fostered by many schools today? ...
>
> The question you'd ask in assessing any potential
> investment, then, is not "Will it make me money?"
> but "Will it beat my hurdle rate?"—Will any invest-
> ment yield a stronger return than the best alternative
> investment you know you could make?[84]

I would suggest that Charlotte Mason would express something similar about narration. The question we should ask ourselves about any of our disciplinary devices that we might plan for a particular lesson is, "Will it beat the hurdle rate of narration?" That will ensure that our analytical exercises are of a high quality indeed.

84. Ibid.

CHaPTER FIVE

....

THE NARRATION LESSON AND THE TRIVIUM

I n a 2018 ACCS conference presentation entitled "Charlotte Mason and the Trivium," I argued that this flexible lesson plan structure does a particularly good job of embodying the trivium, or three-fold path, of the classical tradition.

To see how, consider the five steps of Charlotte Mason's narration lesson as corresponding to training in one of the trivium arts of grammar, dialectic, or rhetoric.

1. First Little Talk—Pre-Grammar
2. Reading of a Rich Text—Grammar
3. Narration—Pre-Rhetoric
4. Second Little Talk—Dialectic
5. Response—Rhetoric

In order for these designations to make sense, we need to envision the trivium arts according to their historical meaning rather than how we have come to think of them as modern subjects. First of all, we need to note that the ancient conception of the trivium was not as discrete subjects, for which the term science (Latin "*scientia*" or Greek "*episteme*") would have been used, but as arts: complex language skills built on an imitative foundation.[85] The difference between mastery of an art and a science is not insignificant because the focus of a science is on demonstrable knowledge whereas an art focuses on the capacity to produce something in the world.

This distinction goes all the way back to Aristotle when he defined the intellectual virtue of "art" as a "state of capacity to make [something], involving a true course of reasoning" (1140[a].31), whereas "knowledge" or "science" is a "state of capacity to demonstrate" (1130[b].10).[86] In other words, someone who is skilled in the art of basket-weaving has the ability to weave a basket correctly, based on prior experience and practice and according to the actual nature of the materials and the needs of a basket ("a true course of reasoning"). On the other hand, someone who has knowledge, or has learned a particular "subject" or "science", is able to show or demonstrate that knowledge, whether through inductive or deductive reasoning.

The liberal arts are a special case since the product they create is not a basket or building, a painting or a sword, but the "works of reason," like "arguments, poems, and proofs" as Clark and Jain mention.[87] The products are the artifacts of communication in the world. Historically, grammar included not just analyzing parts of speech and syntax but the entire

85. Compare Clark and Jain's comments in *The Liberal Arts Tradition*, 2nd ed., 40:
The ancients and medievals had clear distinctions between imitation, art, and science. All things, whether poems, statues, or swords, were made by either imitation or art. A science, on the other hand, was a body of knowledge organized by principles of demonstrative reason, requiring a knowledge of causes but producing nothing on its own—the knowledge was enough. . . . The arts were different. One of the ancient patterns in education was that *imitation precedes art*. An art could only be attained from an extensive foundation in action and imitation forming cultivated habits.
86. Aristotle, *Nicomachean Ethics* VI.4, 1140a from *The Complete Words of Aristotle*, vol. 2, The Revised Oxford Translation (Princeton University Press, Princeton: 1984), 1800, 1799. Clark and Jain primarily cite Aquinas for this distinction, but he would have been dependent on Aristotle. Augustine's *De Musica* (esp. I.4), which they also cite, further establishes this distinction while clarifying that one person could be both skilled in the art of music and at the same time have knowledge about music in the mind.
87. Clark and Jain, *The Liberal Arts Tradition*, 41.

work of reading and interpretation. This can be seen in the derivation of both the Latin and Greek terms for the English word "letter." The Greek word "*gramma*" leads to "*grammatike*"; the Latin "*littera*" becomes "*litteratura*."[88] So the product of grammar is, most directly, the mental act of putting together the letters on a page into words and sentences. In a similar vein, dialectic was the art of discerning the truth through discussion and reasoning, the product being the dialogue or debate itself that two or more people would produce. And rhetoric was the art of knowledgeable and persuasive discourse, the product being the persuasive speech or essay.[89]

In each of these trivium arts, as complex skills of language, an extensive foundation in imitative practice is required along with coaching by a teacher competent in the art and opportunities for rational reflection on the art.[90] Once we have conceived of the trivium arts in this broader, more holistic way, the value of the narration lesson structure in the previous chapter becomes evident. The trivium is not taught only in distinct subjects throughout the day, but its core skills must be embodied and actively coached in *all* the subjects studied.

But how are we to do so practically? Because I have already

---

88. Quintilian identified "litteratura" as the Latin equivalent to "grammatike" in his *Institutes of Oratory*, 2.1.4. The common Latin term for "to read" ("legere") also is regularly glossed as "to collect" or "to gather" probably indicating a historical understanding of reading as collecting letters into words. Given that spacing was not introduced until the late Roman period, this becomes even more of a clear act of interpretation. (The Greek *anaginoskein*, literally "to know up or again" probably points in a similar direction of bringing to mind the right word.)

89. Compare Clark and Jain's revised section on the trivium in *The Liberal Arts Tradition*, which describes grammar as "being at home in language, [and] learning from the authors" (47); dialectic as "finding arguments, following questions, [and] demonstrating reasons" (55); and rhetoric as "leading souls to truth with wisdom and eloquence" (60).

90. On this point, Clark and Jain cite Augustine's *De Musica* for support of the idea that reason must be joined with imitation for the attainment of art (ibid.). Aristotle's definition of the intellectual virtue of "art" could have been equally adduced: "a state of capacity to make [something], involving a true course of reasoning" *Nicomachean Ethics* VI.4, 1140a in *The Complete Words of Aristotle*, vol. 2, 1800.

tackled narration in detail in chapter two, I will simply address the first little talk, which I like to call the set-up, the reading of a rich text, the second little talk or discussion and the response to new content. In the next chapter, we will discuss in more detail how narration itself relates to the liberal arts tradition, including the trivium.

The First Little Talk or Set-Up—Pre-Grammar

The first little talk or set-up aims to prepare students for a high-comprehension reading of the text. It is thus preparatory for the act of reading and interpretation (hence pre-grammar) and provides important background knowledge required to read well.[91] The basic principle is as follows:

> *The more students understand during the single reading of the text, the higher quality their narrations will be and the more knowledge they will gain from them.*

This principle deserves some explaining because it serves as a guide for all the suggestions that follow.

When students attend to a text and then narrate it, they are engaged in the process of articulating as much as they can take in of the text. If a student encounters a text that is far above his comprehension—so far, in fact, that nothing but the barest facts could be discerned—his narration is likely to contain only those bare facts. Of course, this assumes the student has had the opportunity to develop fluency in narration, so it is not the mental skill of narrating that is getting in the way but the challenges of the content itself.

When we read texts, our mind goes through a rapid and complex process in which it attempts to grasp the meaning

---

91. This stage, therefore, roughly corresponds to the preparation stage of the mimetic sequence of teaching as espoused by the CiRCE Institute.

of the communication through determining relevance to all the categories of meaning we *already* know.[92] There is always more to any piece of communication than meets the eye. There are inferences and assumptions that guide the reader in comprehending the meaning of the story and in piecing together the relevant details into a coherent narrative. For any text, there are hundreds of potential ways to misunderstand it, if you are unaware of various details of context, background knowledge, or the exact meanings of words.

In other words, when our students read and narrate, they are engaged in the complex process of interpretation. Their minds automatically attempt to discern the meaning of the text in context based on what seems to make most sense to them. If the text contains several words that are new to them, they will try to infer their meaning based on pieces of the communication puzzle that they *do* know. These inferences are sometimes successful and sometimes quite incorrect (because of no fault of their own). They simply don't have the right knowledge base; they have not been adequately prepared to comprehend this text.[93]

While this may seem overly philosophical, simply ask a child to narrate a challenging text and you will see it on display.

---

92. In what follows, I am referencing in a broad way the insights of relevance theory specifically and hermeneutics generally. However, these comments are not dependent on any one school of thought in communication theory or hermeneutics to my knowledge but accord with standard insights into the complexities of reading and interpretation (primarily from the field of biblical studies, my own area of training). Resources that I have personally profited from and may be beneficial to the reader include Anthony Thiselton's *Hermeneutics: An Introduction* (Grand Rapids: Eerdmans, 2009), and Jeannine Brown's *Scripture as Communication* (Grand Rapids: Baker Academic, 2007).

93. Compare the insights of John Milton Gregory's *The Seven Laws of Teaching*, Chapter four "The Law of the Language," in which he claims that "the language used in teaching must be common to teacher and learner" (54). Interestingly, he clarifies that "this discussion of language is not to be interpreted as an encouragement to the teacher to become a lecturer before his class," thus making the thrust of his work as a whole parallel to the concerns of Charlotte Mason, his older contemporary across the sea.

Possible misunderstandings abound in rich texts. Hearing students make these minor errors through the process of narration is an incredibly valuable gold-mine of insight for the teacher. Through these moments, a teacher can develop a detailed mental repository of the types of things that students are likely to misunderstand and therefore how best to set up future lessons. In this way, narration provides a source of data for the teacher—a formative assessment, to recall Chapter One—informing the teacher in how to better train students in the art of grammar.

But it is also true that some errors of interpretation are unnecessary. If it is possible to correct those errors afterward, it is also possible for the skilled teacher to head them off beforehand and be sure they never arrive. That is the goal of the first little talk or set-up. It includes raising expectation or putting students in the right frame of mind to eagerly receive the new content—but it should also involve priming them for *correct* interpretation (pre-grammar).

> Of course, it is possible to correct such errors afterward, and one of the reasons the practice of narrating as a class is so valuable is that any given child is unlikely to make exactly the same errors as other students. Thus, there is a natural process of self-correction involved in reading and narrating together. This is further improved through a well-led discussion afterwards, which we will unpack later.

An illustration may help at this point. Say you are reading the story in 1 Samuel where David was anointed by Samuel as king over Israel. Perhaps you suspect that some of your students may not know what the word "anoint" really means, both in terms of what it physically entails (pouring oil on the head), and what it implies (setting apart a person for some sacred service to God, like that of a priest, prophet or king). You could proceed in your lesson in one of two ways.

Either you could read the text to the students first, during which they may be perplexed at the significance of the anointing, and even if they tell back the word "anoint" they may still make various mistakes in their narration, because the attendant details did not make sense to them without that background knowledge. And then afterward you could correct their misunderstandings and fill them in with the background knowledge of the word "anoint" during a discussion. This would be all well and good and a very useful lesson for the students.

On the other hand, you could anticipate students' possible misunderstandings by filling them in on the background information of "anoint" ahead of time, thus priming them to interpret the text well. Their narrations will then likely be of higher quality and will include details connected to the act of anointing with higher precision. Then your ensuing discussion will not have to focus on correcting errors of interpretation and can instead go in any number of different directions, such as pursuing the significance of God's choice of David. In both options, you will have helped students learn important background knowledge about anointing, but in the second option, you have gained time in the last part of the lesson to develop other deeper ideas as well.

When I phrase the scenario like that, it may seem obvious that it is better to head off possible misunderstandings before they arise, but this is the exact opposite of what we often do in practice. Perhaps this is because it is hard work to imagine what our students know and do not know about the text in front of us. It requires both a trained sensitivity and a fair amount of experience with students of the age and developmental level that we teach. But this is no excuse for not committing to the process with the goal of making the most of every opportunity for training our students in the art of reading and interpretation.

This, then, is the first call for skill development on the part of the teacher. The first little talk or set-up is the teacher's opportunity to prepare her students for as high quality a reading of the text as possible.[94] This is a key way to optimize the learning that occurs through narration. While narration is a powerful enough practice that simply reading and narrating with no preparation would be fairly effective over the long haul, we can do better through pursuing excellence in setting students up for interpretive success.

The exciting thing about this process is that interpretive success builds upon itself. The more students successfully interpret texts (the art of grammar), the more knowledge they gain through narration. The more knowledge they have stored away through narrating challenging texts in many different subject areas, the more background knowledge they have stored away that will help them successfully interpret other texts.[95] In this way, they are learning how to learn, because their knowledge gained from reading helps them to read new texts better and better.[96]

---

94. This goal of the set up might be paralleled by Quintilian's concern that the grammar teacher engage in the "illustration of the poets" (1.4.2) and "explanations of historical points, which must be sufficiently minute, but not carried into superfluous disquisitions; for it will suffice to lecture on facts which are generally admitted, or which are at least related by eminent authors" (1.8.18), *Institutes of Oratory*, 20, 49.

95. In this way, the intellectual virtues of "art" and "knowledge" are mutually beneficial and interpenetrating. This does not diminish the value of the classical distinction between an art and a science, because the distinction is meant to clarify the most important part of a whole for a particular purpose. As John Milton Gregory comments in *The Seven Laws of Teaching*, 11:

> These two great branches of educational art—training and teaching—though separable in thought, are not separable in practice. We can only train by teaching, and we teach best when we train best. Training implies the exercise of the powers to be trained; but the proper exercise of the intellectual powers is found in the acquisition, the elaboration, and the application of knowledge.

96. Obviously, this references Dorothy Sayers' famous claim in "The Lost Tools of Learning," but a couple of generations earlier Gregory had already stated that "the first object of teaching is to communicate such knowledge as may be useful in gaining other knowledge, to stimulate in the pupil the love of learning, and to form in him the habits of independent study," ibid., 10.

The Reading of a Rich Text—Grammar

The reading itself might seem simple and straightforward, but here, too, there are a variety of possible ways to read a text that might have an impact on students' comprehension.

As mentioned above, the teacher might read aloud, direct students to read aloud, or have the students read silently either in class or at home. While some decisions are obvious enough— like that students should only transition to reading aloud themselves or reading silently as they grow in ability with the technical aspects of reading—others are less obvious.

In the first place, the teacher should read the text aloud artfully, with appropriate phrasing, mood, and emotion. This is especially important with texts that push students' reading ability. It's the perfect moment for a teacher to act like an ancient *grammaticus* and model the art of beautiful and effective public reading.[97] Without teachers modeling this standard, students won't become the readers they could, whether aloud or silently in their minds.

Even if you feel unqualified to do this, just bringing some intentionality to your practice of reading aloud can go a long way. We're not looking for reading that is overly expressive, but the energy and voice modulation of normal speech will help students interpret well. You may be wondering when you should read yourself rather than calling on students; some texts will present innumerable difficulties for even the experienced student reader. With foreign or hard-to-pronounce names, it is preferable for the teacher to look them up and practice them beforehand. If students are going to read aloud, then these words should be written on the board, and the whole class should practice pronouncing them in chorus after the teacher during the set-up stage.

---

97. As Quintilian says of the teaching of the grammarian: "For not only is the art of writing combined with that of speaking, but correct reading also precedes illustration, and with all these is joined the exercise of judgment." (1.4.3), *Institutes of Oratory*, 20.

> ## Vocal Technique in Reading Aloud
>
> Many modern Americans tend to press down on their vocal chords, artificially lowering their voice and creating a gravelly sound that is unpleasant and unhealthy. I owe this observation to my wife, Ashley, an experienced singer with her master's in voice performance. What she would recommend is thinking lighter and slightly higher than what feels normal to most of us. Then, aim to express the meaning of the text as clearly as possible. This requires a little bit of reading ahead to feel out where the emphasis of a sentence should go and how it flows grammatically and syntactically.

Poetry lends itself to artful reading aloud, and short lyric poems, especially, due to their compactness, should be read aloud multiple times by both the teacher and the students before narration begins. I've found that high school students understand Milton's *Paradise Lost* and other linguistically difficult texts best when the books are read aloud to them. Such texts contain so many new words and expressions as well as features of ornate style and elaborate syntax that students are trying to process too much to read well *and* comprehend at the same time. Also, these Great Books have a verbal cadence that even our most advanced students are simply not yet capable of reproducing with their current verbal imagination.

After all, silent reading is a strange modern phenomenon, and for it to be done most effectively, a person needs to be able to imagine the spoken word well-phrased in one's mind. Our current practice in which we simply send students home to read on their own, without strong training in public reading beforehand, is probably what is causing a lot of the comprehension challenges we see in our oldest students. Reading aloud is not just an important practice for young students.

It goes without saying that some practice in quality silent reading in class is advisable for older students if for no other reason than its usefulness for most standardized tests—let alone the fact that it is the standard modern method of reading in work or daily life.[98] For this very reason, I would not expect anyone reading this book likely to go to the extreme of adopting reading aloud exclusively.

As students progress to reading aloud for themselves, that, too, provides opportunities for training them in the art that has been modelled for them. The main requirement here is plenty of coached practice in the art. As Quintilian comments:

> Reading remains to be considered. Only practice can teach a boy to know when to take breath, where to divide a verse, where the sense is concluded, where it begins, when the voice is to be raised or lowered, what is to be uttered with any particular inflection of sound, or what is to be pronounced with greater slowness or rapidity, with greater animation or gentleness than other passages. There is but one direction, therefore, which I have to give in this part of my work, namely, that he may be able to do all this successfully, let him understand what he reads.[99]

Notice how concerned Quintilian is with the details of elegant and beautiful reading, almost as if it were an end unto itself. At the same time, he acknowledges the importance of "understanding" or proper interpretation to make this possible. A student cannot read aloud a text excellently when it is beyond his comprehension.

Encouraging students to give a dramatic flair to their reading should generally help and not harm their ability to comprehend and narrate. The goal is for students to bring the text to life and engage with its content fully. Narration is not a memorization

---

98. Silent reading was a standard option in Charlotte Mason's schools, as can be deduced from her comment in *School Education*, "There is much difference between intelligent reading, which the pupil should do in silence, and a mere parrot-like cramming up of contents" *Ambleside Online*, https://www.ambleside-online.org/CM/vol3complete.html#179; accessed February 2020.
99. Quintilian, *Institutes of Oratory*, 1.8.1–2, 46.

game; it is the act of recalling what was memorable. If the text is a play, or the passage has dialogue, students can be assigned parts to read. The act of reading itself should be as delightful and interesting as possible. You want to catch the soul of a book. The reading should aim to breathe life into the words on the page.

The Second Little Talk or Discussion—Dialectic

In this part of the lesson, the teacher guides the students in thinking carefully and deeply about what they have read, either to understand it more fully or to apply it to broader ideas and concepts. Thus, it represents an ideal opportunity to train them in the art of discovering the truth through conversation and reasoning.

Teachers who are accustomed to classroom discussion will find some pleasant surprises in the discussion which follows narration. First, the fact that narration has just aired all the important details of the text prevents a lot of the sidetracks that often derail classroom discussions. Misunderstandings by some students can suck up a lot of time from more in-depth inquiry. While these still occasionally surface, they are greatly reduced in number and frequency in the post-narration discussion.

Second, since factual information has mostly been dealt with in the narration process, the discussion should focus not on assessing students' comprehension or on minor details but on the ideas and broader significance of the content.

For instance, a historical text about medieval kings could lead into a discussion of leadership and various virtues and vices that are on display. A John Donne poem could lead into a discussion of how he uses surprising metaphors and images for salvation and what that communicates about the nature of Christian experience. A biology class could discuss the ethics of mapping the human genome and genetic engineering or engage in a lab that leads them through a course of reasoning to discover what they read about for themselves.

Many schools tout the integration of all subjects, but few have a regular mechanism for integrating the insights of various subjects in a way that is natural and not artificially constructed. In the discussion after narration the students themselves will often make connections to the ideas in other subjects and books they have read. Of course, the teacher can initiate such connections herself, but the strength of this integration method is that it carries the genuine vivacity of real life. When a student in history makes a connection to a principle discussed in Bible class earlier that week, the artificial tang that unfortunately hangs on other teacher-led methods is entirely absent.

Other than the obvious task of preparing good discussion questions, the teacher should act as a coach, training students in the art of discerning the truth, holding out for real and deep insights, occasionally pushing students' thinking by playing devil's advocate, and enforcing a respectful and fruitful dialogue between peers. Being a dialectician is, as Plato's dialogues illustrate, the art of asking the right question, so the teacher should model a spirit of creative, genuine, and thoughtful inquiry.[100]

One simple way to begin the process of discussion with students is to ask one of them, "What strikes you?" or "What idea stands out to you?" In discussing the importance of ideas in her sixth Volume of *Toward a Philosophy of Education*, Charlotte Mason says:

> What is an idea? we ask, and find ourselves plunged beyond our depth. A live thing of the mind, seems to be the conclusion of our greatest thinkers from

---

100. Compare Clark and Jain's comments in *The Liberal Arts Tradition*, 56: "Importantly, we find as well that the goal of dialectic is not to have all the right answers but to learn to ask the right questions. Socrates models for us this notion of dialectic as the art of asking good questions in his relentless practice of refining and reframing the question."

Plato to Bacon, from Bacon to Coleridge. We all know how an idea "strikes," "seizes," "catches hold of," "impresses" us and at last, if it be big enough, "possesses" us; in a word, behaves like an entity.[101]

There are many profitable ways of leading discussions, but this beginning tactic of opening it entirely up to the inspiration of a student can often lead just as surely into the heart of a text as some elaborate question we may devise. A justification for this approach can be found in David Hicks' definition of dialectic as "simply the form of the activity of thinking: the mind's habit of challenging the thoughts and observations originating inside and outside itself and of engaging in a desultory dialogue with itself until the issues are resolved."[102] Forcing students to externalize that thinking process allows the teacher to guide and shape it from within rather than impose an opinion from outside.

Modern learning science has confirmed the value of this verbal dialectic as what it calls "elaboration." As the authors of *Make It Stick* explain:

Elaboration is the process of giving new material meaning by expressing it in your own words and connecting it with what you already know. The more you can explain about the way your new learning relates to your prior knowledge, the stronger your grasp of the new learning will be, and the more connections you create that will help you remember it later.[103]

101. Mason, *Toward a Philosophy of Education*, 84.
102. David Hicks, *Norms and Nobility: A Treatise on Education* (New York: University Press of America, 1999), 24–25. He goes on to explain the value of externalizing this in a discussion, as illustrated by Socrates: "By bringing the form of man's mental activity to light, Plato enables man to include others in his dialogue with himself and turns dialectic into an activity of learning (or knowledge)."
103 Brown, Roediger III, and McDaniel, *Make It Stick*, 5.

One common beginner's error in leading discussions is to ask students questions that are too complicated. If a student has to work very hard just to interpret what you are getting at with your discussion question, then it is a poorly worded question. Socrates' questions may have been deep and intellectually demanding, but they were always simply phrased and to-the-point. Beware the temptation to sound intellectual; aim for clarity of thought and expression.

Responding to New Knowledge—Rhetoric

Lastly, we address other responses to knowledge that Charlotte Mason had earlier called "disciplinary devices."[104] It should be remembered that with older children especially, the step of narration itself could be replaced entirely by the response. An analytical assignment that "tabulates" the knowledge in the book and sets the students' minds busily to work digesting and incorporating it into a broader framework is itself a sufficient method of learning. And, in fact, this accords well with the modern research on retrieval practice, which can be done effectively in any number of different ways.[105]

However, a response can also follow the normal narration process and act as a secondary application of knowledge that helps students develop their thinking in complexity and insight.

For example, after reading tale after tale of *King Arthur and the Knights of the Round Table*, a class could work together to

---

104. Mason, *School Education*, 181 Ambleside Online https://www.amblesideon-line.org/CM/vol3complete.html#181, accessed February 2020.
105. In the terminology of modern learning science, the response to new knowledge might also constitute the development of mental models; the authors of *Make It Stick* claim that "people who learn to *extract the key ideas from new material and organize them into a mental model* and connect that model to prior knowledge show an advantage in learning complex mastery" (Brown, et al., 6).

brainstorm a list of all the types of things that might occur in an Arthurian tale (e.g., an encounter with dwarves, trickery by Morgana, a jousting contest with knights of various colors of armor, damsels in distress, etc.). In so doing, they analyze the genre of an Arthurian tale for representative conventions of the plot, characters, and settings. Then they could be tasked with producing their own Arthurian tale that follows the conventions they identified.

In this way, students create their own rhetorical composition based on their knowledge of a great work of literature. This rhetorical and poetic task beats most creative writing assignments because it includes as its foundation genuine imitation and a wealth of knowledge (gained through narration and analysis). The example above is a real life one I have used with sixth graders, and it is not only an effective assignment that demonstrates real mastery of the content, but it is also one of the students' favorite activities all year.

Not all responses have to be this elaborate. They could be as simple as writing a paragraph in response to a question about the text, a lab report after a science experiment, or a student's presentation of their viewpoint in front of the class. The class could work together on formulating an outline of the text, or each student could work on their individual summary or *precis*. Using words might not even be necessary. In Charlotte Mason's school, younger students often drew illustrations of key moments in a narrative or engaged in a dramatic performance of the story.[106] There is no limit to the legitimate ways to respond to text.

The only important caveat is that students should have the knowledge necessary to complete the assignment effectively. If students read a short text about a Civil War battle and are then asked to write letters home as if they were a soldier, but they are

---

106. In *Know and Tell,* Karen Glass cites an article from *The Parents' Review* in 1899 describing such an "impromptu dramatic performance" which received some "candid criticisms afterward" and took only about five minutes (48).

not given a wealth of historical detail about what life was like for soldiers at the time or the types of things that Civil War soldiers actually wrote home, then the creative exercise is likely to be nothing more than an exercise of unsubstantiated imagination. Students asked to complete this sort of assignment will often remember more of the ahistorical "facts" they made up than anything that they read, leaving them more ignorant of history than they were before the lesson (because they now think they know things about the Civil War that are in fact untrue).

Teachers who implement narration should not feel that their work is done once they've got the basics of narration in place in their classrooms. There is a lifetime of study involved in setting up students to interpret each new text correctly, managing the reading optimally, then directing genuine inquiry and responses to the deep ideas of the texts. Aiming to excel at leading the whole lesson will also prevent the charge that narration is boring or simplistic. Narration is rather a core step in a fully orbed process of learning from texts.

And while books may be old-fashioned in some educators' minds, it is hard to argue with the academic product that this sort of lesson produces in the long-term: intelligent and knowledgeable young men and women who know how to learn for themselves, can listen to others patiently, discuss ideas rationally, and speak and write persuasively.

In this chapter, we have discussed the lesson plan that naturally surrounds narration: the set-up or first little talk and the reading of a rich text before it; the second little talk and response to new knowledge after it. Even if students are doing the work of learning through narration, there is still so much for the teacher to do in order to help the students get the most out of their attention to the valuable content.

CHAPTER SIX

....

NARRATION IN THE LIBERAL ARTS TRADITION

N ow that we've stepped back from narration proper to see how it fits within a broader lesson structure, we can focus our attention once again on narration to evaluate how it relates to the liberal arts tradition in more detail. We've seen how the narration lesson is ideally suited for training students in the arts of the trivium. But how does narration itself as a practice relate to all that the classical renewal has rediscovered about education so far?

If you'll recall, I concluded the first chapter with a discussion of narration as a traditional teaching exercise drawn from the rhetorical tradition. From Quintilian to the late nineteenth century, there are scattered references to the practice of having students narrate content in an extended way. However, it's important to remember that this was used as a preliminary exercise or *progymnasmata*, limited in scope and frequency. Narration in the liberal arts tradition did not reach nearly the consistency or exactness of Charlotte Mason's method, and so she is rightly credited with the development of narration as a core learning tool.[107]

Since the details of the practice of narration as advocated for

107. See Introduction for the full discussion of this discovery.

here are relatively new in the history of classical education, it's worth stepping back to consider how they relate to the rest of the tradition. Moreover, given that this book is a guide for applying the practice in the classical school, the issue of coherence is particularly relevant. Can narration be understood as a natural development within the liberal arts tradition or does it represent, in any way, a concession to modern education's attempt to separate itself from that tradition?

To avoid making this analysis unnecessarily long and complicated, we will primarily rely on Kevin Clark and Ravi Jain's *The Liberal Arts Tradition: A Philosophy of Christian Classical Education* (revised edition) for our exploration. Their PGMAPT paradigm (Piety, Gymnastic, Music, Liberal Arts—trivium and quadrivium—Philosophy, and Theology) is an ideal comparison point for the practice of narration as a core pedagogical strategy, both because of its holistic and well-documented vision, but also because it is the most recent attempt within the classical renewal movement to sketch out the philosophy of the liberal arts tradition comprehensively.

Piety and Gymnastic

Clark and Jain have drawn attention to the importance of early training in piety, or "the proper love and fear of God and man," and gymnastic, or "disciplined physical training."[108] Modernism's fantasy of a value-neutral education finds no support within the traditions of the Ancients and Medievals. Likewise, the importance of the body is neglected by modern education's dichotomy between the mind and the body. On first glance, narration may seem net-neutral on these important issues, but in fact, narration can function as one important strategy for embodying the principles of piety and gymnastic in the modern classical school.

---

108. Clark and Jain, *The Liberal Arts Tradition*, 18, 26.

First of all, narration is an inherently pious act. It involves the posture of humility and attention to a traditional text that is accorded value. In fact, narration assumes that what a child most needs to do with the text is not to criticize it, nor to dissect it and discard it, nor even to use it as a springboard for their own insights and creative expressions. Instead, what a child should do, first and foremost, with an accepted text is simply to receive it and tell it back faithfully. In a way, narration is the act of tradition itself, handing on (from the Latin *"tradere"*) what you have received from others as a valuable inheritance.

The narration lesson of Charlotte Mason focuses the class's attention not on the teacher—she is simply a tradent, one who passes on an authority—nor on the child as the creator of meaning, as in some postmodern educational philosophies, but on the text.[109] The goal of the lesson is a proper hearing of—and submission to—the text as a source of learning and wisdom.

There are few places more important for this training in piety than with scripture itself, and so it is not surprising to hear Moses commanding a similar sort of diligence in retelling the instructions given to him from God in the famous *Shema*:

> Hear, O Israel: The Lord our God, the Lord is one. You shall love the Lord your God with all your heart and with all your soul and with all your might. And these words that I command you today shall be on your heart. You shall teach them diligently to your children, and shall talk of them when you sit in your house, and when you walk by the way, and when you lie down, and when you rise. (Deut 6:4-7 [ESV])

109. For the term "tradent" I am dependent on John H. Walton and D. Brent Sandy's *The Lost World of Scripture: Ancient Literary Culture and Biblical Authority* (Downers Grove: IVP Academic, 2013), 25ff.

In commending the way of piety, love to the one true God, Moses has specifically called for the oral recitation and discussion of the instructions given to him within the households of the covenant community.[110] Since these originally oral instructions have been preserved as a text, the most natural way to follow Moses' command would be to read aloud, narrate, and discuss them in our families and Christian schools. As Christians this extends from Deuteronomy and the Pentateuch to all of scripture, which should be read and recited in our homes, churches, and schools.

As far as gymnastic training, here too the bodily habit of focus and attention are crucial for a student's development. Although telling back texts does not train students' bodies in the higher athletic skills, it does develop bodily habits that support higher learning. As Clark and Jain comment,

> We are unions of body and soul, and these two elements are interrelated in everything we do. On the one hand, the physical conditions required for learning are obvious, even if at times neglected. Imagine attempting to read a piece of literature with a headache, or when overly tired; it is exceedingly difficult at best. Clearly, reading is a work of both mind and body.[111]

The active nature of telling back a text balances out the more passive act of reading itself. Even the movements involved in verbalizing to another student engage the body in rehearsing the content. Moreover, narration trains students in the bodily habit of an attentive posture. And as Charlotte Mason claims,

---

110. The word translated "teach... diligently" is best rendered as to "repeat" or "recite." The word may be *šānan* meaning most often "to sharpen," though the meaning "to incise or engrave or impress" has been suggested here (see D. Kellerman, *"šānan; šenînâ," Theological Dictionary of the Old Testament*; Grand Rapids: Eerdmans, 2006; 15:343-344). However, even when this is maintained, a metaphorical meaning similar to *šānâ* II ("to repeat") is adopted.

111. *The Liberal Arts Tradition*, 30.

"the highest intellectual gifts depend for their value upon the measure in which their owner has cultivated the habit of attention."[112] When a student is clear about the task he must complete when he finishes reading, he has been given the stimulus necessary to give his full attention to the text.

So, while narration is not directly necessary either for an education in piety or for gymnastic training, it is a viable tool for training students in a pious attitude toward texts, especially Scripture, and in the bodily habits of mental focus.

Musical Education

Narration has more of a direct relationship with what Clark and Jain term "musical education," meaning not primarily instruments and singing, but a pre-critical, affective encounter with inspiring subjects.[113] We should think of the nine Muses of Greek mythology who were born of memory and inspired such subjects as epic and lyric poetry, tragedy and comedy, various instruments, singing and dance, and also history, geography and astronomy. They note that "in classical antiquity, a major portion of the education of children ... consisted of physical training, singing, memorizing poetry, acting/imitating, drawing, sculpting, learning of the deeds of the great men of the past, reading great literary works, and experiencing and observing the natural world."[114] The goals of such musical education were "tuning hearts to the real," passing on the tradition's values and cultivating the moral imagination and trained sentiment that C. S. Lewis so adamantly defended in *The Abolition of Man*.

All of the subjects and activities recommended as musical education had their place in Charlotte Mason's grand scheme

---

112. Mason, *Home Education*, 97.
113. See *The Liberal Arts Tradition*, 24–27 and 32–35.
114. Ibid., 26.

of education. For example, recitation involves the memorization of poetry, a key element in Mason's classroom. Likewise, studies focused on appreciation and joyful discovery of the world of art and nature, like nature study and picture study (the study of the paintings or great artists); these "subjects" held a prominent place in her educational model. But even here, narration often functioned as an imitative, affective way to engage with these subjects. As mentioned above, the act of retelling involves the speaker in the beauty of the content, whatever it is. Even telling back about the burr-oak tree after a descriptive reading or time spent observing it in close detail connects the student personally to the tree in a way that simple observation does not.

What's more, narration begins in musical education—not grammar—as a natural, pre-critical mode of assimilating musical subjects from fable to poetry, history, music, and astronomy. Before students can read aloud effectively for themselves (grammar), they can hear and tell.[115] While they are still learning the rudiments of reading skills, they can assimilate aurally much more challenging material than they can read for themselves. Therefore, narration as a learning tool necessarily begins *before* grammar, understood historically as the complex skill of reading and interpretation.

Because narration involves that pre-critical engagement with musical subjects, it also provides the imitative foundation for the language arts of the trivium. Narration provides a seamless transition between early training of musical education and the

---

115. Charlotte Mason is explicit about this in *Home Education*, 155:
> When the child is six, not earlier, let him narrate the fairy-tale which has been read to him, episode by episode, upon one hearing of each; the Bible tale read to him in the words of the Bible; the well-written animal story; or all about other lands from some such volume as *The World at Home*. . . . The seven-years-old boy will have begun to read for himself, but must get most of his intellectual nutriment, by ear, certainly, but read to him out of books.

Our schools will not likely want to start reading that late, but for her time such recommendations would have been more normal.

ongoing work "of forming the heart, the sense of wonder, and the affections," as the liberal arts of language and number begin to be honed.[116] Mind and heart are integrated through the synthetic work of narration.

The Liberal Arts—Grammar

Within grammar—the art of reading and interpretation—narration optimally supports the transition from oral language to written discourse. Narration is able to do this because it ties the child's oral expression and aural reception abilities (i.e., their learned capacity to hear and speak) closely to their acquisition of literacy.[117] Through the close attention that anticipates being called on to narrate, the written word on the page is connected to what students hear and see as they read along with the class. Then the narration from memory further solidifies the knowledge they have gained by honing the art of interpretation through a feedback loop that connects the simple process of hearing and telling to a check on their understanding of the text as told.

So, while narration does not constitute the language art of *grammatike*, it is a practice that, when employed regularly after

---

116. Clark and Jain, *The Liberal Arts Tradition*, 35.

117. As a highly literate society, we tend to be unaware of the ways that the technology of "writing restructures consciousness"; as Walter Ong explains in a chapter of that name in *Orality and Literacy*, 82:

> Oral speech is fully natural to human beings in the sense that every human being in every culture who is not physiologically or psychologically impaired learns to talk. Talk implements conscious life but it wells up into consciousness out of unconscious depths, though of course with conscious as well as unconscious co-operation of society ... Writing or script differs as such from speech in that it does not inevitably well up out of the unconscious. The process of putting spoken language into writing is governed by consciously contrived articulable rules: for example, a certain pictogram will stand for a certain specific word, or a will represent a certain phoneme, b another, and so on.... Technologies are not mere exterior aids but also interior transformations of consciousness, and never more than when they affect the word.

reading, ensures that students attend carefully to the written text. Since the heart of the art of grammar is this act of reading text, students will grow in their skill in grammar at an improved rate because of narration. By tying the spoken and written word so closely, students' acquisition of literacy is accelerated. Likewise, because the narration offers this feedback loop on interpretation, students' reading comprehension in various genres and subject areas is advanced more quickly. While reading comprehension quizzes and discussions might clarify for students certain details, narration commends itself as an altogether more efficient tool for quick feedback as students and teacher become an interpretive community, reading and applying the text together.

These benefits of narration should not at all be taken to dismiss or undervalue the sub-skills of phonetics, spelling, parts of speech, and other reading skills as well as the rules and categorizations of language that are regularly labeled "grammar" today. All these isolated pieces of grammatical knowledge really do advance students' understanding of language and their literacy. But such sub-skills serve the end of proper interpretation of texts, and once learned, they naturally fall into the background of the act of reading itself. Narration functions as the glue that holds the pieces together by ensuring a quality reading.

The Liberal Arts—Rhetoric

The very act of telling for an audience regularly provides students with active practice in the art of speaking well.[118] The fact that students regularly serve as an audience for another narrator provides them with many opportunities as rhetorical critics; since they themselves attended to the content the first time through, their brains naturally enter the analytical mode as they compare their own memory of the content in all of its exact detail, as well as its beauty and eloquence, with the telling they are hearing from another student. This process eases naturally into rhetoric proper as students acquire reasoning about the art and apply that to their imitative foundation. Plus, the art of telling itself is a subset of rhetoric; there is a reason *narratio* was a standard ingredient in almost every sort of rhetorical address.[119]

The telling of stories and connected trains of thought is a *sine qua non* for the true rhetorician. Often, older students who are initiating their study in rhetoric proper are hamstrung by the fact that they lack the confidence and practice to speak in a fluent and connected format before an audience. John Locke, the British enlightenment philosopher, noted a similar fault in the gentlemen of his day, who, in spite of their "classical education" had not received real training in the art of rhetoric. For, he says, they "cannot so much as tell as a story as they should, much less speak clearly and persuasively in any business." He lays the blame for this on their education and then diagnoses the fault:

---

118. Charlotte Mason explicitly recognized this connection; see, for instance, *Toward a Philosophy of Education*, 98: "They [students who read and narrate great authors in English, like Bacon, Milton and Shakespeare] will welcome the preparation for public speaking, an effort for which everyone must qualify in these days, which the act of narration offers."

119. Note for instance the comments of George Kennedy, a leading expert on the rhetorical tradition, *Classical Rhetoric and Its Christian and Secular Tradition*, 27: "By at least the first century B.C., virtually all Greek and Roman students were practiced in progymnasmatic exercises in grammar or rhetorical schools. They learned a highly structured, approved way of narrating, amplifying, describing, praising, criticizing, comparing, proving, and refuting something."

They have been taught rhetoric but yet never taught how to express themselves handsomely with their tongues or pens in the language they are always to use: as if the names of the figures that embellished the discourses of those who understood the art of speaking were the very art and skill of speaking well. This, as all other things of practice, is to be learned not by a few, or a great many rules given, but by exercise and application according to good rules, or rather patterns, till habits are got and a facility of doing it well.[120]

The rhetoric teachers of Locke's day had been treating the art of rhetoric as if it were a science that could be mastered through acquiring knowledge about the art: various names of figures of speech and rules for types of speeches. But without the facility with language based in practice and cultivated habits, all of it was useless!

So Locke commended early exercises in narration by making "children, as soon as they are capable of it, often to tell a story of anything they know, and to correct at first the most remarkable fault they are guilty of in their way of putting it together."[121] Then he recommended curing the next important fault and so on until they are well capable of telling. At this point, they should be required to write them, and he recommends Aesop's fables as a particularly good starting place for this sort of exercise.[122]

As mentioned in the Introduction, Charlotte Mason likely drew her inspiration for the practice of narration from John Locke (or

---

120. John Locke, *Some Thoughts Concerning Education* and *Of the Conduct of the Understanding*, edited with Introduction by Ruth W. Grant and Nathan Tarcov (Indianapolis: Hackett, 1996), 141. *Some Thoughts Concerning Education* was first published in 1693.
121. Ibid.
122. Ibid. Locke is very likely dependent on Quintilian here, as a number of his reflections on education mirror the early chapters of his *Institutes of Oratory*.

Quintilian directly).[123] By beginning young children in the practice of narration and keeping it as an educational staple throughout their education, the fluency and confidence necessary for both speaking and writing eloquently will be so ingrained in the rhetoric student ahead of time that their progress will be that much faster. Where only natural public speakers would have thrived, a high level of rhetorical skill can be attained by the average student when narration has provided that basic foundation.

The Liberal Arts—Dialectic

Narration has less of a close connection to the art of dialectic or logic.[124] However, in familiarizing a student with a wide range of content and ideas, it accustoms her mind to begin thinking out ideas to their logical conclusions. One of Charlotte Mason's most important requirements for books was that they be "living," or, we might say, idea-rich. When children are regularly reading such literature, the natural outcome is thought.

How many a student has come home to a parent after a day full of narrating living books, only to pose some deep philosophical quandary to their parent as if out of nowhere! A little probing reveals that it was a single thought from one of their books that day, which

---

123. One clue pointing in this direction is her mention of reading and narrating "the well-written animal story" in the chapter introducing narration for the first time in *Home Education*, 155. Aesop's fables is the most well known set of animal stories, and Charlotte Mason accorded it an honored place in the PNEU curriculum throughout her tenure, as can be evidenced by her statement in her final volume, published shortly before her death, *Towards a Philosophy of Education*, 139, "Aesop's Fables, too, are used with great success, and are rendered, after being once heard, with brevity and point, and children readily appropriate the moral."

124. This is not the place to delve into the debate about dialectic vis-a-vis logic as the true trivium art. However, my approach here of privileging dialectic warrants a brief explanation. Logic is a refinement of the dialectical art into rules and principles, as well as an exploration of the nature of thought itself; therefore, it bridges into the science of the same name. Dialectic has a more ancient and basic claim in the spoken method of discussion modelled by Socrates. As the more primary human art, therefore, dialectic deserves pride of place in a PK–12 pedagogy.

their mind had been spinning on, until the dialectic of their mind burst forth the question to the parent. Of course, this is not the technique of dialectical reasoning, but it is the imitative foundation of it. And the practice of narrating logical and philosophical texts most certainly has the power to join reason with imitation according to the requirement of the liberal arts.[125]

The Liberal Arts—Quadrivium

The quadrivium (or four-fold path) represents the mathematical arts of arithmetic, geometry, music, and astronomy, embracing both traditional mathematics and science in its observational aspect.[126] In earlier chapters, I have already alluded to ideas for using narration in math and science courses: rehearsing a geometric proof just demonstrated by a teacher on the board, completing a similar math problem to one that has been illustrated, and the write up of a lab report after a science experiment.

These last two examples are not new, but tried and true methods of mathematics instruction. In such cases, we are merely drawing attention to how these exercises require the student to retell a story or re-enact a process that they have witnessed. And while problem solving and lab reports are not sufficient in and of themselves to accomplish the goals of "wonder, work, wisdom, and worship," nevertheless they grow in pedagogical value when we see them as part of the storytelling of the quadrivium arts.[127]

After all, there is a reason that the trivium arts of language

---

125. See Clark and Jain, *The Liberal Arts Tradition*, 40-41.
126. Clark and Jain call astronomy and music "middle sciences utilizing mathematics" and "those which joined mathematics with natural philosophy." Astronomy, in particular, "was the best example of a mathematical system devised to contain a vast amount of observational data," ibid., 83.
127. Ibid., 69. See also 109ff.

precede the numerical arts of the quadrivium, and that is because, for all their well-acknowledged power, quantification itself must be nested within a qualitative framework. Numbers themselves require interpretation in the terms of value and worldview. Perhaps, if we were to entwine again the quadrivium with the trivium, we would be one step closer toward addressing the "disengagement" and "fragmentation" of the modern world.[128] As Clark and Jain put it, "What might it look like to once again comprehend in a single vision what modernity has separated into the objective and merely quantitative realm of scientific knowledge and the radically subjective qualitative realm of love, meaning and value?"[129]

While these reflections ultimately concern philosophy or the sciences (next section), they suggest that the use of narration in the quadrivium could be one piece of the puzzle that moves math and science in the right direction. For example, situating math and science instruction within the story of mathematical and scientific discovery would provide a host of opportunities for the use of narration in the math or science classroom. Clark and Jain envision science classes "tracing the developments of a scientific idea through various new observations, mathematical innovations, and philosophical or theological convictions." In this way, science "recovers a kind of story or narrative—not a purely literary narrative, but a technical narrative."[130] If their vision were enacted, narration both of the stories of discoverers and of the equations and experiments they used could be profitably incorporated into the normal curriculum.

Clark and Jain are not the first to suggest a return to the

128. Colin E. Gunton, *The One, the Three and the Many: God, Creation and the Culture of Modernity*, The Bampton Lectures 1992 (Cambridge: Cambridge University Press, 1993), 13–14, 114–115. The former he attributes to Charles Taylor, and on the latter, he states "that the cultural disarray that is so marked a feature of our times derives from our failure to integrate or combine the different objects of human thought and activity: in brief, science, morals and art."
129. Clark and Jain, *The Liberal Art Tradition*, 106.
130. Ibid., 124, 125.

narrative of math and science. In the early twentieth century, Charlotte Mason had already advocated for a "literary narrative" of scientific discovery, even if she did not go as far as Clark and Jain in advocating for the technical side of things:

> Books dealing with science as with history, say, should be of a literary character, and we should probably be more scientific as a people if we scrapped all the text-books which swell publishers' lists and nearly all the chalk expended so freely on our blackboards. The French mind has appreciated the fact that the approach to science as to other subjects should be more or less literary, that the principles which underlie science are at the same time so simple, so profound and so far-reaching that the due setting forth of these provokes what is almost an emotional response; these principles are therefore meet subjects for literary treatment ....[131]

For Mason, the commitment to "literary" books, what she elsewhere called "living books," came out of her conviction that the mind naturally responds with attention to beautiful, vigorous writing. Of course, if literary science books told the story of science, it would also be easier for students to be asked to narrate in science class.[132] But we should also notice that Charlotte Mason doesn't just want the story to be told without students understanding the principles. In fact, it is the "due setting forth" of scientific principles which "provokes what is almost an emotional response."

---

131. Mason, *Toward a Philosophy of Education*, 218–219. While she did not recommend the same for mathematics instruction, her principles might suggest some movement in this direction.

132. A botanist of my personal acquaintance, who spent some time as a science instructor at the school where I served as Academic Dean, grew up in France, and he has recounted fondly how in France pre-collegiate math was taught to him in this same way: where the story of great mathematicians and their discoveries were given a prominent place in the mathematics curriculum just as in science.

This literary and technical narrative of science should not crowd out the place for wonder, for laboratory, for manipulatives, and for hands-on discovery, especially early in a child's development. Mason also advocated for nature studies, in which "children keep a dated record of what they see in their nature note-books" while going on a "nature-walk" one afternoon a week.[133] Her goal was to train children in the love of nature and the skill of "interested observation."

Interestingly, Barbara Oakley, a professor of engineering at Oakland University and a Fellow the American Institute for Medical and Biological Engineering, has endorsed both the stories of discovery and the importance of retrieval practice for math and science learning in a recent book directed at students: *A Mind for Numbers: How to Excel at Math and Science (Even If You Flunked Algebra)*. She recounts research from the journal *Science*:

> Students studied a scientific text and then practiced it by recalling as much of the information as they could. Then they restudied the text and recalled it (that is, tried to remember the key ideas) once more. ... In the same amount of time, *by simply practicing and recalling the material*, students learned far more and at a much deeper level than they did using any other approach, including simply rereading the text a number of times or drawing concept maps that supposedly enriched the relationships in the materials under study. This improved learning comes whether students take a formal test or just informally test themselves. (emphasis original)[134]

133. Mason, *School Education*, 236–237. *Ambleside Online*, https://www.amblesideonline.org/CM/vol3complete.html#236, accessed February 2020.
134. Barbara Oakley, *A Mind for Numbers: How To Excel at Math and Science (Even If You Flunked Algebra)* (New York: TarcherPerigee, 2014), 70-71. The study she cites was published in *Science* in 2011 by J.D. Karpicke and J.R. Blunt, "Retrieval practice produces more learning than elaborative studying with concept mapping," 331, 6018: 772–775.

These considerations should put to rest the assumption that math and science stand outside the purview of the practice of narration, even if it does not answer all the particulars of application, which I will leave to those with more experience in teaching science and math to answer.

Philosophy or the Sciences

Narration also connects a student through the trivium and quadrivium arts to the world of the sciences. While simply accepting an authority and telling it back does not represent the culmination of scientific knowledge (*scientia* or *episteme*), still a great part of expert knowledge relies on the ability to accept, digest, and build upon the foundation of other authorities. The capacity to narrate furthers the progress of the advancing scientist (in the fullest sense of the word whether in the natural, moral, or divine realms) to an incredible degree. We are all standing on the shoulders of giants, and now more than ever before, a great part of reasonable demonstration of causes is learned through reading, with comprehension and lasting memory, the causal demonstrations of others. Advancing science relies on the knowledge of those who have come before. And the highest culmination of the scientist, the discovery of genuinely new knowledge, again in whatever domain, depends upon a mind full of all the knowledge currently available up to that point, reaching out into the new.

But we don't need to think of philosophy or science as necessitating an expert's creation of new knowledge. In fact, one of the clearest ways that Charlotte Mason can be seen to embrace the liberal arts tradition is in how she ordered her curriculum. In her final volume, *Towards a Philosophy of Education*, published in 1922, a year before her death and representing her most mature thought, Mason deliberately adopted the trifold division of Medieval philosophy. She orders her discussion of curriculum under the knowledge of God, the knowledge of man, and the knowledge of the universe, thereby echoing the old division between divine philosophy or science, moral philosophy, and natural philosophy. Interestingly, though, in Mason's thinking, the acquisition of such knowledge does not await the mastery of the liberal arts, as if only the university student could begin attaining knowledge in these areas. Instead, these "three sorts of knowledge [are] proper to a child, the knowledge of God, of man, and of the universe."[135]

She connects this innovation to a criticism of the modern "utilitarian" focus in education, trying to "make a boy's education bear directly on his future work," or "to educate young people for their uses to society," rather than opening each child to all the relationships with God, others, and the world that he was born into as a person created in the image of God.[136] Closing off to children knowledge in any area is ultimately a failure to acknowledge the "natural law or inherent principle according to which a child's course of studies should be regulated." Of course, this is not really an argument with the liberal arts tradition, which always engaged many subjects from the earliest ages, even though it retained the fullness of "philosophical knowledge" as only attainable by the mature *magister artium* ("the master of the arts").

Mason felt that her discovery of narration as a core tool of education made possible a new educational development within the liberal arts tradition, in which knowledge of God, man, and the universe would come to play a fuller role for every young child:

---

135. Mason, *Towards a Philosophy of Education*, 122.
136. Ibid., 119.

The days have gone by when the education befitting either a gentleman or an artisan was our aim. Now we must deal with a child of man, who has a natural desire to know the history of his race and of his nation, what men thought in the past and are thinking now; the best thoughts of the best minds taking form as literature, and at its highest as poetry, or, as poetry rendered in the plastic forms of art: as a child of God, whose supreme desire and glory is to know about and to know his almighty Father: as a person of many parts and passions who must know how to use, care for, and discipline himself, body, mind and soul: as a person of many relationships,—to family, city, church, state, neighboring states, the world at large: as the inhabitant of a world full of beauty and interest, the features of which he must recognise and know how to name, and a world too, and a universe, whose every function of every part is ordered by laws which he must begin to know.[137]

The scope of such an educational program is truly breathtaking. Mason's enthusiastic hope was that the practice of narration had opened a way to the feasible attainment of so lofty a mission. In her experience, the practice of narration ensured that "the knowledge of children so taught [was] consecutive, intelligent and complete as far as it goes, in however many directions."[138]

---

137. Ibid., 120. In the previous context, Mason had referred to teaching "those things which, according to Locke, it is becoming for a 'gentleman' to know on the one hand, and, on the other, the arts of reading, writing and summing, that he may not grow up an illiterate citizen" (119); here, therefore, she is likely commenting on the limits of a noble's education and a bare liberal arts education. In a way then, her whole project coheres with the thesis of Clark and Jain's *The Liberal Arts Tradition* in restoring the full scope and holistic nature of the classical tradition.
138. Ibid., 121.

Theology

There is in Charlotte Mason, however, an implicit theological critique of the Aristotelian conception of philosophical science. The issue especially concerns our conception of knowledge and what constitutes knowledge. For example, many philosophers would define knowledge as "justified, true belief," a definition that draws from the Aristotelian tradition that required a demonstrable knowledge of causes. While Mason does not attack this idea directly, she prefers a Medieval and Renaissance theological focus on the doctrine of revelation.

In a chapter of her second volume, *Parents and Children*, which is entitled "The Great Recognition," Mason explicates the glorious fresco in the Spanish Chapel of the Church of Santa Maria Novella, in which a dove descends on, not only the theological sciences, but also the seven liberal arts:

> The great recognition that God, the Holy Spirit, is Himself personally the imparter of knowledge, the instructor of youth, the inspirer of genius, is a conception so far lost to us that we should think it irreverent to conceive of the divine teaching as co-operating with ours in a child's arithmetic lesson, for example. But the Florentine mind of the Middle Ages went further than this. It believed, not only that the seven liberal arts were fully under the direct outpouring of the Holy Ghost, but that every fruitful idea, every original conception, whether in Euclid, or grammar, or music, was a direct inspiration from the Holy Spirit, without any thought at all as to whether the person so inspired named himself by the name of God, or recognized whence his inspiration came. All these seven figures [of the liberal arts] are those of persons whom we should roughly class

> as pagans and whom we might be lightly inclined to
> consider as outside the pale of divine inspiration. It
> is truly difficult to grasp the amazing boldness of this
> scheme of the education of the world which Flor-
> ence accepted in simple faith."[139]

Charlotte Mason connects this idea of revelation or inspiration to her discussion of ideas in her final volume. She draws extensively from Samuel T. Coleridge's philosophical and theological reflections on the subject. She also quotes from Isaiah 28 to the effect that, even in the case of the ploughman or the sower sowing seed, "his God doth instruct him aright and doth teach him," implying that the ideas "of great inventions and discoveries" as "of practical ideas" are "presented to chosen minds by a higher Power than Nature herself."[140]

While Mason does not develop in detail her conception of divine revelation or inspiration as part and parcel of the acts of teaching and of learning, it was a matter of core conviction for her, such that she often emphasized the teacher's participation with the Holy Spirit. Narration, then, was not merely a human exercise, but was a participation with the divine process of revelation to each individual child, imparting truths that had already been revealed to some earlier mind. These captain figures of the liberal arts and sciences may have drunk first hand from the fount of wisdom, just as prophets and apostles were made the recipients of special revelation. But every person can receive the inheritance of such truth through the personal and intimate revelatory work of the Holy Spirit.

Charlotte Mason believed that narration was more than just an effective learning strategy. Narration is how a person's mind

---

139. As quoted in Cholmondeley, *The Story of Charlotte Mason*, 50 (caption altered by the author). Mason is indebted to John Ruskin's *Mornings in Florence* for her interpretation of the fresco.

140. Mason, *Toward a Philosophy of Education*, 85, quoting from the authorized version at the first and then Coleridge's *Method* in the final quotation.

appropriates, through the mediating influence of the Holy Spirit, the ideas and truths that have been made available to us in the tradition of wisdom and knowledge. Narration is a spiritual exercise and a gift of grace.

Afterword

NEXT STEPS

*P*erhaps the best payoff for adopting narration is the increased joy that students experience in learning. Engaging so deeply with content inspires deeper relationships with the matter of knowledge itself. Students are invested in their learning and therefore naturally express their feelings (both positive and negative) about what they are reading. In her third volume *School Education*, Charlotte Mason borrowed a phrase from Matthew Arnold to describe this goal of true classical education: knowledge "touched with emotion."[141]

Now that you've read about the process of implementing narration and its connection to the liberal arts tradition, the most important next step is to begin implementing it in your own classroom. See for yourself the changes in classroom culture that result from moving to a narration-based lesson structure.

The journey of implementing narration may be initially difficult, but it is well worth it. And it is a journey that is best traveled with others. If you are a teacher, share this book with others at your school—with your principal or another

---

141. *Ambleside Online*, https://www.amblesideonline.org/CM/vol3complete.html#220, accessed February 2020.

administrator. If you're an administrator, consider taking your whole school on this journey together. The power of narration to raise both the academic standards and the joy in learning of a whole school is hard to beat.

BIBLIOGRAPHY

Aristotle. *Nicomachean Ethics.* In *The Complete Words of Aristotle,* vol. 2, The Revised Oxford Translation. Princeton: Princeton University Press, 1984, 1800, 1799.

Brown, Jeannine. *Scripture as Communication: Introducing Biblical Hermeneutics.* Grand Rapids: Baker Academic, 2007.

Brown, Peter, et al. *Make It Stick: The Science of Successful Learning.* Cambridge, MA: Belknap, 2014.

Caldecott, Stratford. *Beauty in the Word: Rethinking the Foundations of Education.* Tacoma, WA: Angelico Press, 2012.

Cholmondeley, Essex. *The Story of Charlotte Mason (1842-1923),* 2nd ed. London: Child Light, 2000.

Clark, Kevin, and Ravi Jain. *The Liberal Arts Tradition: A Philosophy of Christian Classical Education.* Revised ed. Camp Hill, PA: Classical Academic Press, 2019.

Cooper, Elaine, ed. *When Children Love to Learn: A Practical Application of Charlotte Mason's Philosophy for Today.* Wheaton: Crossway, 2004.

Gibbs, Joshua. *Something They Will Not Forget: A Handbook for Classical Teachers.* Concord, NC: CiRCE, 2018.

Glass, Karen. *Know and Tell: The Art of Narration.* 2018.

Gregory, John Milton. *The Seven Laws of Teaching.* Moscow, ID: Canon Press, 2017. Reprint from 1st edition, 1886.

Gunton, Colin E. *The One, the Three and the Many: God, Creation and the Culture of Modernity.* The Bampton Lectures 1992. Cambridge: Cambridge University Press, 1993.

Hicks, David. *Norms and Nobility: A Treatise on Education.* Lanham, MD: University Press of America, 1999.

Kellerman, D. "*šānan; šᵉnînâ,*" in *Theological Dictionary of the Old Testament* 15:343-344. Grand Rapids: Eerdmans, 2006.

Kennedy, George A. *Classical Rhetoric and its Christian and Secular Tradition from Ancient to Modern Times.* second ed., Chapel Hill and London: University of North Carolina, 1999.

Lemov, Doug. *Teach Like a Champion 2.0: 62 Techniques That Put Students on the Path to College.* San Francisco: Jossey-Bass, 2015.

Lewis, C. S. *The Abolition of Man.* New York: HarperCollins, 2001.

Locke, John. *Some Thoughts Concerning Education and Of the Conduct of the Understanding.* Edited with Introduction by Ruth W. Grant and Nathan Tarcov. Indianapolis: Hackett, 1996. First published 1693.

Macaulay, Susan Schaeffer. *For the Children's Sake: Foundations of Education for Home and School.* Wheaton, IL: Crossway, 1984.

Mason, Charlotte. *Home Education.* Radford, VA: Wilder, 2008.
_____. *Parents and Children.* Vol. 3 of the AmblesideOnline Annotated Charlotte Mason Series. Accessed February 2020 at httpp://www.amblesideonline.org/CM/toc.html#2.

_____. *School Education.* Vol. 3 of the AmblesideOnline Annotated Charlotte Mason Series. Accessed February 2020 at https://www.amblesideonline.org/CM/toc.html#3.

_____. *Towards a Philosophy of Education.* Radford, VA: Wilder, 2008.

Oakley, Barbara. *A Mind for Numbers: How to Excel at Math and Science (Even If You Flunked Algebra).* New York: TarcherPerigee, 2014.

Ong, Walter. *Orality and Literacy: The Technologizing of the Word.* London and New York: Methuen, 1982.

Plato. *The Collected Dialogues of Plato, Including the Letters.* Edited by Edith Hamilton and Huntington Cairns, translated by Lane Cooper. Bolingen Series LXXI. Princeton: Princeton University, 2005.

Quintilian. *Institutes of Oratory.* Translated by John Selby Watson, edited by Curtis Dozier and Lee Honeycutt. Creative Commons, 2015.

Scott, Fred, and Joseph Denney. *Elementary English Composition.* Boston and Chicago: Allyn and Bacon, 1900. Reprint available through Palala, 2015.

Thiselton, Anthony. *Hermeneutics: An Introduction*. Grand Rapids: Eerdmans, 2009.

Walton, John H., and D. Brent Sandy. *The Lost World of Scripture: Ancient Literary Culture and Biblical Authority*. Downers Grove: IVP Academic, 2013.

Whitman, Glenn, and Ian Kelleher. *Neuroteach: Brain Science and the Future of Education*. Lanham, MD: Rowman and Littlefield, 2016.

FOR MORE SUPPORT

....

Educational Renaissance exists to promote a rebirth of ancient wisdom about education in the modern era. I or one of my colleagues would love to arrange a visit to your school to train you and your teachers in the practice of narration. There's nothing like sitting in training sessions and experiencing the power of narration as a learning tool for yourself. We have found that teachers are best prepared to implement narration effectively for the long haul when they are taught how through the principles outlined here, narration and all!

For testimonials of teachers and administrators who have experienced this training, check out our narration training page! Share the challenges and joys of your narration journey on our Facebook page. Don't try to go it alone. Instead, tell the story of narration to your colleagues and friends.

Please visit <u>educationalrenaissance.com</u> to learn more.

About the Publisher

....

The CiRCE Institute is a non-profit 501(c)3 organization that exists to promote and suport classical education in the school and in the home. We seek to identify the ancient principles of learning, to communicate them enthusiastically, and to apply them vigorously in today's educational settings through curricula development, teacher and parent training, events, multimedia resources, and book publishing.

Learn more at www.circeinstitute.com or on
Facebook or Instagram @circeinstitute.

Also Availalbe from CIRCE

How to Be Unlucky: Reflections on the Pursuit of Virtue
by Joshua Gibbs

Something They Will Not Forget: A Handbook for Classical Teachers
by Joshua Gibbs

The 25th: New and Selected Christmas Essays
by Joshua Gibbs

Tales of Wonder, Volume I

Tales of Wonder, Volume II

*Mere Motherhood: Morning Times, Nursery Rhymes,
and My Journey toward Sanctification*
by Cindy Rollins

*The Lawgivers: The Parallel Lives of Numa Pompilius
and Lycurgus of Sparta as Told by Plutarch*
Translated by David and Scot Hicks

30 Poems to Memorize (Before Its Too Late),
Edited by David Kern

The Acts of The Apostles: A Latin Reader
by Dale A. Grote, PhD

The Lost Tools of Writing, Levels I, II, and III

The Journey Home: A Guide to Homer's Odyssey

The Space Between: A Guide to Homer's Iliad